SQL Primer

An Accelerated Introduction
to SQL Basics

Rahul Batra

Apress®

SQL Primer

Rahul Batra
Gurgaon, Haryana, India

ISBN-13 (pbk): 978-1-4842-3575-1   ISBN-13 (electronic): 978-1-4842-3576-8
https://doi.org/10.1007/978-1-4842-3576-8

Library of Congress Control Number: 2018947350

Managing Director, Apress Media LLC: Welmoed Spahr
Acquisitions Editor: Jonathan Gennick
Development Editor: Laura Berendson
Coordinating Editor: Jill Balzano

Cover designed by eStudioCalamar

Cover image designed by Freepik (www.freepik.com)

Distributed to the book trade worldwide by Springer Science+Business Media New York, 233 Spring Street, 6th Floor, New York, NY 10013. Phone 1-800-SPRINGER, fax (201) 348-4505, e-mail orders-ny@springer-sbm.com, or visit www.springeronline.com. Apress Media, LLC is a California LLC and the sole member (owner) is Springer Science + Business Media Finance Inc (SSBM Finance Inc). SSBM Finance Inc is a **Delaware** corporation.

For information on translations, please e-mail rights@apress.com, or visit http://www.apress.com/rights-permissions.

Apress titles may be purchased in bulk for academic, corporate, or promotional use. eBook versions and licenses are also available for most titles. For more information, reference our Print and eBook Bulk Sales web page at http://www.apress.com/bulk-sales.

Any source code or other supplementary material referenced by the author in this book is available to readers on GitHub via the book's product page, located at www.apress.com/9781484235751. For more detailed information, please visit http://www.apress.com/source-code.

Printed on acid-free paper

To Mum and Dad.

Table of Contents

About the Author

Rahul Batra was first introduced to programming in 1996 in GWBASIC, but he did not seriously foray into it until 2001 when he started learning C++. Along the way, there were dabblings in many other languages like C, Ruby, Perl, Python, and Lisp. He has worked with databases such as PostgreSQL, Sybase ASA, and SQLite. He is passionate about sharing knowledge, especially with those who are just starting out. Rahul currently lives and works in Gurgaon, India.

About the Technical Reviewer

Stefan Ardeleanu was born in Bucharest, Romania, in 1967. He graduated Math and Philosophy, and he was a math teacher for 10 years. Afterwards, he started a career in software development. He felt attracted by databases from the beginning so his entire career in software industry has been related to databases and, especially, to database development and design.

Stefan Ardeleanu is a database specialist, a database architect and developer, working for many years under various systems as Oracle, SQL Server, DB2, and PostgreSQL. He has experience in OLTP and Data warehouse and replication systems.

Stefan is a passionate SQL guy, and he was able to develop and improve a specific style of development. This style is reflected in his various projects, including replication systems and data migration systems, where this style is highly required.

Acknowledgments

I got into computing early, when I was around 12 years old. In those days, buying a personal computer was an expensive affair. Especially in a developing country like India where the computer revolution was slow to reach the household level. I owe a debt of gratitude to my parents and my sister for providing me with a PC. Without it, I certainly would not have had as much passion for the field as I do now. Thank you for your unwavering belief in me.

My wife not only acted as an editor for the early drafts of this text but also took the lion's share of taking care of our child while I was writing the book. Thank you for your patience and encouragement.

Completing a book is rarely an individual effort. I thank the team at Apress for working with me to bring this to fruition. Thank you, Jonathan and Jill for taking a chance on me and keeping me focused. Thank you, Stefan and Laura for combing through the text and improving the finished product immensely.

Finally, thanks are in order to my early readers who suggested improvements and caught errors – Keith Thompson, Nathan Adams, Paul Guilbault, Jim Noh, and Sean Farrell.

Introduction

I wrote the predecessor text to this book in late 2012 and put it on the Internet hoping someone would find it useful. There was enough response that I continued writing and we have this book as a result. There have been lots of changes and additions over time, but the core aim remains the same – a brief introduction to SQL assuming no prior experience in it.

After reading this text, the reader should be able to recognize the parts of queries they encounter and even be able to write simple SQL statements and queries themselves. The book, however, is not intended as a reference work or for a full-time database administrator since it does not have exhaustive topic coverage.

The book is written in a linear fashion – you start from Chapter 1 and work your way forward. Being example heavy, I hope readers are able to jump to certain topics and get a quick recap. The examples are worked out in PostgreSQL and SQLite, but the goal is to remain DBMS implementation agnostic as far as possible.

I encourage you to tinker with the statements and queries as you progress through the book. Also, be sure to check out the appendices for book recommendations to help you dig deeper in the world of SQL and databases.

Your questions, comments, criticism, encouragement, and corrections are most welcome and you can e-mail me at rhlbatra@hotmail.com.

CHAPTER 1

An Introduction to SQL

Modern society is driven by data. Whether it is at a personal level, like a notebook containing scribbled notes; or at a countrywide level like Census data, it has permeated all our workflows. There is always a growing need to efficiently store and organize it so that meaningful information can be extracted out of raw data.

A **database** is nothing but a collection of organized data. It doesn't have to be in a digital format to be called a database. A telephone directory is a good example, which stores data about people and organizations with a contact number. A to-do list is also a rudimentary form of a database. With ever-larger amounts of data being collected about even the most mundane of processes, digital databases have become increasingly important since their inception in the 1960s.

Software that is used to manage a digital database is called a *Database Management System (DBMS)*. When you hear someone talking about *PostgreSQL* or *MySQL*, they are referring to a DBMS. A database is what is created when you use the DBMS software to store data about topics that make sense to you or your organization. For example, your company may use *PostgreSQL* to store inventory information about cellular phones – the product that you sell. In this case, you have created an inventory *database* using *PostgreSQL* as your DBMS.

© Rahul Batra 2018
R. Batra, *SQL Primer*, https://doi.org/10.1007/978-1-4842-3576-8_1

The Relational Model and SQL

Data comes in myriad shapes and sizes, and every context generates data in a different way. The data generated by a bank keeping a record of account balances is different from keeping track of members of a family tree. But for a DBMS to provide uniform data management and reporting capabilities, we must adhere to a data organization structure or *data model*.

The most prevalent database organizational model is the *Relational Model*, developed by Dr. E. F. Codd in his groundbreaking research paper – *A Relational Model of Data for Large Shared Data Banks* in 1970.[1] In this model, the data to be stored is organized in a tabular format with rows and columns. Each row inside a table represents a distinct record with the column headings specifying the corresponding type of data stored. This is not unlike a spreadsheet where the first row can be thought of as column headings and the subsequent rows storing the actual data.

A database would typically consist of more than one table, each with different column headings. There may be certain columns that are common between tables, but this is a topic we will approach later in the book.

---

[1]Codd, E. F.; "A Relational Model of Data for Large Data Banks," *Communications of the ACM,* vol 13, no 6, June 1970, https://www.seas.upenn.edu/~zives/03f/cis550/codd.pdf

Question   What does the word *relational* in relational database mean?

It is a common misconception that the word relational implies a relationship between the tables. A relation is a mathematical term that is roughly equivalent to a table itself. When used in conjunction with the word database, we mean to say that this particular system arranges data in a tabular fashion.

A possible origin of this misconception might have been the *set relation* command in *dBase*, a DBMS from the 1980s. That command indeed was used to create linkages between tables, but it has nothing to do with relational theory.

SQL stands for **Structured Query Language**, and it is the de facto standard for interacting with relational databases. Almost all database management systems you'll come across will have an SQL implementation. SQL was standardized by the American National Standards Institute (ANSI) in 1986 and has undergone many revisions, most notably in 1992 and 1999. However, all DBMS's do not strictly adhere to the standard defined but rather remove some features and add others to provide a unique feature set. Nonetheless, the standardization process has been helpful in giving a uniform direction to the vendors in terms of their database interaction language.

While SQL is a computer language, it is not like the other programming languages that you may have heard of like Python or C. Such programming languages are generic in nature, suitable for a wide variety of tasks from programming basic calculating systems to advanced simulation models. SQL is a special purpose query language meant for interacting with relational databases. It has no use other than this context.

This does not mean that it is the only database query language to exist. In the 1980s, another language called *QUEL* from *Ingres* was fairly popular, but the standardization effort around SQL cemented its position. In recent years, we have seen a large number of non-relational databases being developed under the umbrella term of *NoSQL*. Most of their query languages, however, bear some resemblance to SQL even though their data model varies significantly from the relational model.

Advantages of Using SQL

- It is *standardized* – no matter which relational database you choose, it will have an SQL query interpreter built in. The sheer popularity of SQL makes it worth everyone's time who interacts with a data system.

- It has a reasonable English-like syntax. None of the painstaking detail of programming languages like C or Java have to be specified when using SQL. It is concise, easy to understand, and easy to write database queries with. It is *declarative* in nature, meaning you only have to declare what you want to achieve rather than going over the steps to achieve the results.

- It allows a uniform way to query and administer a relational database. Many of the database administration commands are standard SQL commands making the transfer of skills much easier.

- It is *mature* – SQL has been around for over 35 years. While many new features have been added to it, the core of SQL has largely been unchanged. You can derive a lot of utility knowing a few basic SQL concepts and commands, and they will serve you well into the future.

SQL Commands Classification

SQL is a language for interacting with databases. It consists of a number of commands with further options to allow you to carry out your operations with a database. While DBMS's differ in the command subset they provide, usually you would find the classifications below.

- **Data Definition Language (DDL)**: *CREATE TABLE, ALTER TABLE, DROP TABLE, etc.* These commands allow you to create or modify your database structure.

- **Data Manipulation Language (DML)**: *INSERT, UPDATE, DELETE.* These commands are used to manipulate data stored inside your database.

- **Data Query Language (DQL)**: *SELECT.* Used for querying or selecting a subset of data from a database.

- **Data Control Language (DCL)**: *GRANT, REVOKE, etc.* Used for controlling access to data within a database, commonly used for granting user privileges.

- **Transaction Control Commands**: *COMMIT, ROLLBACK, etc.* Used for managing groups of statements as a unit of work.

Besides these, your database management system may give you other sets of commands to work more efficiently or to provide extra features. But it is safe to say that the ones above would be present in almost all DBMS's you encounter.

Explaining Tables

A *table* in a relational database is nothing but a two-dimensional matrix of data where the columns describe the type of data, and the row contains the actual data to be stored. Have a look at Table 1-1 to get a sense of the visualization of a table in a database.

5

Table 1-1. *A Table Describing Programming Languages*

ID	Language	Author	Year
1	Fortran	Backus	1955
2	Lisp	McCarthy	1958
3	Cobol	Hopper	1959

The above table stores data about programming languages. It consists of four columns (id, language, author, and year) and three rows. The formal term for a column in a database is a *field* and a row is known as a *record*.

Note   The example tables in this book primarily deal with programming languages, their authors, and the year they were created. We could have used database query languages, but they are far fewer in number.

Our computer hardware and technologies have changed quite a bit since the 1950s and 1960s, but the early programming languages from that era still have a lasting impact on the programming languages of today. *Lisp* – imagined by John McCarthy in 1958[2] is still alive in the form of *Common Lisp*, *Scheme*, and *Clojure*. Even *Fortran* still sees regular use in scientific computing.

---

[2]McCarthy, John; "Recursive functions of symbolic expressions and their computation by machine, Part I," *Communications of the ACM*, vol 3, issue 4, April 1960, http://jmc.stanford.edu/articles/recursive/recursive.pdf

There are two things of note in the example table. The first one is that the *id* field effectively tells you nothing about the programming language by itself, other than its sequential position in the table. The second is that though we can understand the fields by looking at their names, we have not formally assigned a data type to them, that is, we have not restricted (not yet anyways) whether a field should contain alphabets or numbers or a combination of both.

The *id* field here serves the purpose of a *primary key* in the table. It makes each record in the table unique, and its advantages will become clearer in chapters to come. But for now consider this, what if a language creator made two languages in the same year; we would have a difficult time narrowing down on the records. An *id* field usually serves as a good primary key since it's guaranteed to be unique, but usage of other fields for this purpose is not restricted.

A key concept of tables is that they are conceptual in nature and may not have any bearing upon the actual files where the data is stored. When users create a spreadsheet, they associate a file name with the spreadsheet and place it somewhere on their disk. But relational databases hide all these details from the user. The physical storage of a table on the disk might be to a single file, or to many files, or even have a relationship of storing many tables in a single file. It is the responsibility of your DBMS to provide a way to read and write to tables.

Data Types in SQL

Just like programming languages, SQL also has *data types* to define the kind of data that will be stored in its fields. In the table given above, we can see that the fields *language* and *author* must store English language characters. The *id* and *year* fields both store whole numbers.

The commonly used data types you will encounter in subsequent chapters are shown in Table 1-2.

7

Table 1-2. *Various Data Types in SQL*

Character types	*char, varchar*
Integer values	*integer, smallint*
Decimal numbers	*numeric, decimal*
Date data type	*date*

A string of characters is usually stored in either *char* or *varchar*. The former reserves as much space as you want when you specify the field, but if the value you store in it is shorter, the remaining space is wasted. A *varchar*, however, stands for a varying character and will occupy the exact length of the string, nothing wasted. There is, however, a maximum limit to how long a string value you can assign to such a field, and that is specified during the field definition itself.

```
char(12)
varchar(12)
```

If you store the value 'McCarthy' that is eight characters long, the *char* will store it but waste four characters. The *varchar* will store it as exactly eight characters but the whole dynamism comes at a cost of speed. Nonetheless, the speed difference is small enough that for most scenario's you would see the varying character data type being used.

In case of number values, we get a split across two major classes – *integer* for storing whole numbers and *numeric* for storing number values with a decimal point in them. The ranges and limits of the values being stored in them vary with your choice of DBMS. However, a good rule of thumb to follow is to use the smallest data type that will suffice for the present and foreseeable future of your application.

For example, if I were storing student roll numbers, using a *smallint* would suit just fine. In most implementations, this data type allows a maximum value of 32767, a number I mostly expect to be much greater than the number of students in any class.

Decimal point numbers are trickier to specify. We use the *numeric* data type to fix how large the number could be and how many numbers can occur after the decimal point.

```
numeric(precision, scale)
numeric(5, 2)
```

The total number of digits is specified by the *precision* and the number of digits after the decimal point is represented by *scale*. So in the example given, we would be able to store a number like 999.99 but not any further.

Since data types still vary from a DBMS implementation to another, I suggest you keep your DBMS manual handy. Each implementation gives you many other types to work with, but for our learning purposes, the ones above should suffice.

CHAPTER 2

Getting Your Database Ready

The best way to learn SQL is to practice writing the commands on a real relational database management system. In this book SQL is taught using either one of the following systems: **PostgreSQL** or **SQLite**. The reasons for choosing these DBMS systems are simple – they are free and open source, with availability on most major platforms. PostgreSQL is a full-features enterprise class database management system with a great community. SQLite is a small but robust system that is especially suited for learning purposes. Choose the latter if you are not comfortable with software installations.

However, any relational database product that you can get your hands on should serve you just fine. In some cases, you may already have access to one in your organization, but be sure to ask for permissions to use it for learning purposes. There might be minor incompatibilities between different vendors, so if you choose something else to practice on while reading this book, it would be a good idea to keep the database vendor's user manual handy.

Since this text deals largely with teaching SQL in a product-independent manner, rather than the teaching of a specific DBMS system, details with respect to installation and specific operations of the product will be kept to a minimum. Emphasis is instead placed on a few specific steps that will help you to get working on writing SQL as fast as possible.

© Rahul Batra 2018
R. Batra, *SQL Primer*, https://doi.org/10.1007/978-1-4842-3576-8_2

Using PostgreSQL

The latest version of PostgreSQL as of writing this book was 9.6. You don't absolutely need the latest version; in fact I use version 9.5 in this text.

You can download the latest version of PostgreSQL from *https://www.postgresql.org/download/* for your platform. For the fastest and easiest installation, I would recommend you choose your platform from the *Binary Packages* list. Pre-built binaries mean that you can simply download and install PostgreSQL like any other software using a graphical step-by-step installer.

After choosing your platform, you might still get multiple ways to perform an installation. I'd recommend choosing the graphical installer version from third-party vendors like *BigSQL* or *EnterpriseDB*. I had chosen the *EnterpriseDB* installer for my *Fedora Linux* machine, and a friendly installation procedure popped up when I ran the downloaded file, asking for details like the installation directory (Figure 2-1).

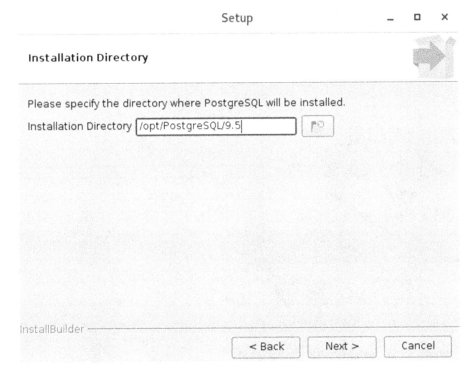

Figure 2-1. *EnterpriseDB PostgreSQL installation wizard*

Some other details will also be asked for, most importantly the port number and password. The default value of 5432 for the port number should suffice. At the end of installation, you would have user named 'postgres' on your system and a working database installation.

You can quickly verify that everything went well using *psql*, which is a command-line utility to interact with your PostgreSQL installation. I am capturing the command and output from my system below (Listing 2-1).

Listing 2-1. Launching the psql shell

```
[~]$ /opt/PostgreSQL/9.5/bin/psql -U postgres
psql.bin (9.5.8)
Type "help" for help.

postgres=#
```

If you get a similar output, you are ready to start using your PostgreSQL installation. If not, I'm afraid you will have to do some digging on your own. You can also choose SQLite, which is discussed in the next section and has a much easier installation procedure.

Using SQLite

If installing PostgreSQL seems like a daunting task, you are in luck. There is a very credible, free alternative database for you to practice on. It is called **SQLite** and its creator D. Richard Hipp has generously licensed it in the public domain. You can download it from the project page at: `https://www.sqlite.org/download.html`

Like the previous section, what you are looking for to get the fastest start is *precompiled binaries* corresponding to your operating system. SQLite is tiny; on most platforms its core engine is less than one megabyte!

If you are using Microsoft Windows, you are looking for the section titled "Precompiled Binaries for Windows." Download the SQLite DLL zip archive, named like *sqlite-dll-win32-x86-xxxxxxx.zip*, which contains SQLite but not a way to interact with it. For that you must download the SQLite shell, named like *sqlite-tools-win32-x86-xxxxxxx.zip*, which will allow us to create and query SQLite databases through the command line.

Extract both these archives into the same directory and you are done installing SQLite. Your folder should now contain at least three files:

- *sqlite3.dll*
- *sqlite3.def*
- *sqlite3.exe*

The last one launches the command shell used to interact with SQLite databases.

If you are on a Linux or MacOS X system, chances are high that you already have SQLite installed. To test this, you can attempt launching the SQLite shell *sqlite3* (Listing 2-2).

Listing 2-2. Launching the sqlite3 shell

```
[~]$ sqlite3
SQLite version 3.13.0 2016-05-18 10:57:30
Enter ".help" for usage hints.
Connected to a transient in-memory database.
Use ".open FILENAME" to reopen on a persistent database.
sqlite>
```

If you get the output as above, you have everything you need to run SQLite. Alternatively, if you get an error message, it means you have to install it yourself. You can either use the similar precompiled binary method for your platform or you could use the system installer.

For systems like Red Hat Enterprise Linux, Scientific Linux, and CentOS, you can use *yum* to install SQLite.

```
# yum install sqlite
```

On a Fedora Linux system, you have to use *dnf* as below.

```
# dnf install sqlite
```

If you happen to use a Debian- or Ubuntu-based system, you can achieve the same result with the following.

```
$ sudo apt-get install sqlite3
```

Once the installation is done, you can verify the installation by launching the SQLite shell as before.

Creating Your Own Database

Database management systems like PostgreSQL allow you to create multiple databases. For practice purposes, it's advisable to create your own database, so that you are free to perform any operations on it.

Most database systems differ in the way they provide database creation facilities. PostgreSQL achieves the same by providing you multiple ways to do this, including through the *pgAdmin III* graphical utility. However, for didactic purposes, we will instead use a command operation to create our database. Open up the *psql* shell and enter the command as below (Listing 2-3).

Listing 2-3. Creating a database in PostgreSQL

```
CREATE DATABASE testdb;
```

The command **CREATE DATABASE** is used to create a database that will serve as a holding envelope for your tables. In the example and output shown above, we created a database called *testdb* for our use. The login user you used while connecting with psql, in most cases *postgres*, is now the owner of this database and has full control of entities within it. This is analogous to creating a file in an operating system where the creator gets full access control rights and may choose to give other users and groups specific rights.

The SQL standard by definition allows commands and keywords to be written in a case-insensitive manner. In this book we will use uppercase letters while writing them in statements, which is a widely accepted practice.

Note   Oddly enough, the SQL standard doesn't include the *CREATE DATABASE* command. In the 1992 standard, aptly named SQL-92, there is a *CREATE SCHEMA* command that was close to the former but not exactly similar.   In modern times, however, databases like *MySQL* treat the two commands as synonyms of each other.

If you are using SQLite, fire up the command shell, and you will be greeted with a text printing version information (Listing 2-4). This is exactly the same message we saw in the previous section when we were verifying our SQLite installation.

Listing 2-4. Opening the SQLite shell

```
SQLite version 3.13.0 2016-05-18 10:57:30
Enter ".help" for usage hints.
Connected to a transient in-memory database.
Use ".open FILENAME" to reopen on a persistent database.
sqlite>
```

Here we enter our .open command to both create a SQLite database or open it in case it already exists.

```
sqlite> .open testdb
```

On a Linux system, you could also simply write the database name after the command of the SQLite shell like below, and you would be able to open the said database.

```
sqlite3 testdb
```

Interestingly, this invocation would not result in creation of *testdb*, it would simply open it if it exists. If you don't perform any other operation and close the shell (Ctrl-D), there would be no *testdb* file on your machine on Linux. On a Windows system, you would get an empty file with a length of 0 bytes.

Table Creation

We have already explored the concept of a table in a relational model. It is now time to create one using a standard SQL command – CREATE TABLE (Listing 2-5).

17

Listing 2-5. General Syntax of a CREATE TABLE statement

```
CREATE TABLE <Table_Name>
(<Field 1> <Data Type>,
 <Field 2> <Data Type>,
 \. \. \.
 <Field N> <Data Type>);
```

This is the simplest valid statement that will create a table for you, devoid of any extra options. We'll further this with clauses and constraints as we go along, but for now let us use this general syntax to actually create the table of programming languages we introduced in Chapter 1 (Listing 2-6).

Listing 2-6. Creating the programming languages table

```
CREATE TABLE proglang_tbl (
id        INTEGER,
language  VARCHAR(20),
author    VARCHAR(25),
year      INTEGER);
```

We have to key this command in PostgreSQL on the `psql` shell. Notice that when we launch the shell, the last line where our cursor waits looks as below:

```
postgres=#
```

This actually means that we are connected to the database named *postgres*, which is something the PostgreSQL installation uses internally for management purposes. We have already created our very own database. Let's switch to that before creating our tables using \c (Listing 2-7).

Listing 2-7. Connecting to a different database in psql

```
postgres=# \c testdb
You are now connected to database "testdb" as user "postgres".
testdb=#
```

Notice that the text on the last line has changed, indicating the current database we are connected to. Now you can key in the table creation statement given in Listing 2-6, and if you don't miss any of the important punctuation or misspell the keywords written in uppercase, your table would be created and the shell would reply simply with:

```
CREATE TABLE
testdb=#
```

A non-successful command would yield an error with a helpful explanation. To see this in action, let's run the exact same table creation command again. The shell would now respond:

```
ERROR:  relation "proglang_tbl" already exists
```

The statement by itself is simple enough since it resembles the general syntax of Listing 2-5. It is interesting to note the data types chosen for the fields. Both *id* and *year* are specified as integers for simplicity, even though there are better alternatives. The *language* field is given a space of 20 characters to store the name of the programming language while the *author* field can hold 25 characters for the creator's name.

The semicolon at the last position is the delimiter for SQL statements, and it marks the end of a statement.

If you are using SQLite, the statement remains exactly the same as Listing 2-6. The only difference being that since an SQLite database is a particular file and you open it when opening the SQLite shell, there is no switching of database required (Listing 2-8).

Listing 2-8. Creating the programming languages table in SQLite

```
[~]$ sqlite3 testdb
SQLite version 3.13.0 2016-05-18 10:57:30
Enter ".help" for usage hints.
sqlite> CREATE TABLE proglang_tbl (
   ...> id          INTEGER,
   ...> language    VARCHAR(20),
   ...> author      VARCHAR(25),
   ...> year        INTEGER);
sqlite>
```

Notice that there is no successful operation message. If all goes well, SQLite shell simply moves on. Just for some experimentation, if we try to create the same table again, we get an error saying:

```
Error: table proglang_tbl already exists
```

which is again a helpful and somewhat friendlier error message.

Inserting Data

The table we have just created is empty so our task now becomes insertion of some sample data inside it. To populate this data in the form of rows, we use the DML command INSERT, whose general syntax is given below (Listing 2-9).

Listing 2-9. General syntax of INSERT INTO TABLE

```
INSERT INTO <Table Name>
VALUES ('Value1', 'Value2', ...);
```

Fitting some sample values into this general syntax is simple enough, provided we keep in mind the structure of the table we are trying to insert the row in. For populating the *proglang_tbl* with rows like we saw in Chapter 1, we would have to use three INSERT statements as below (Listing 2-10).

Listing 2-10. Inserting data into the proglang_tbl table

```
INSERT INTO proglang_tbl
 VALUES (1, 'Fortran', 'Backus', 1955);

INSERT INTO proglang_tbl
 VALUES (2, 'Lisp', 'McCarthy', 1958);

INSERT INTO proglang_tbl
 VALUES (3, 'Cobol', 'Hopper', 1959);
```

If you do not receive any errors from psql or sqlite3 (or the SQL interface for your chosen DBMS), then you have managed to successfully insert three rows of data into your table. Notice how we've carefully kept the ordering of the fields in the same sequence as we used for creating our table. This strict ordering limitation can be removed, and we will see how to achieve that later on.

If you ran these three statements in *psql*, at the end of each executed statement, you would receive a message like:

```
INSERT 0 1
```

indicating a success.

Writing Your First Query

Let us now turn our attention to writing a simple query to check the results of our previous operations in which we created a table and inserted three rows of data into it. For this, we would use a Data Query Language (DQL) command called **SELECT**.

A *query* is simply a SQL statement that allows you to retrieve a useful subset of data contained within your database. You might have noticed the INSERT and CREATE TABLE commands were referred to as statements, but a fetching operation with SELECT falls under the query category.

21

Most of your day-to-day operations in an SQL environment would involve queries, since you'd be creating the database structure once (modifying it only on a need basis) and inserting rows only when new data is available. While a typical SELECT query is fairly complex with many clauses, we will begin our journey by writing down a query just to verify the contents of our table. The general syntax of a simple query is given below (Listing 2-11).

Listing 2-11. General syntax of a simple SQL query

```
SELECT <Selection> FROM <Table Name>;
```

Transforming this into our result verification query is a simple task (Listing 2-12). We already know the table we wish to query – *proglang_tbl* and for our selection we would use * (star), which will select all rows and fields from the table.

```
SELECT * FROM proglang_tbl;
```

The output of this query would be all the (3) rows displayed in a matrix format just as we intended. If you are running this through *psql*, you would get an output similar to the one given below.

Listing 2-12. Verifying the contents of our table in psql

```
testdb=# select * from proglang_tbl;
 id | language |  author  | year
----+----------+----------+------
  1 | Fortran  | Backus   | 1955
  2 | Lisp     | McCarthy | 1958
  3 | Cobol    | Hopper   | 1959
(3 rows)

testdb=#
```

The output from SQLite would be slightly messier at first, but let's fix that one step at a time (Listing 2-13).

Listing 2-13. Verifying the contents of our table in sqlite3

```
sqlite> select * from proglang_tbl;
1|Fortran|Backus|1955
2|Lisp|McCarthy|1958
3|Cobol|Hopper|1959
sqlite>
```

Clearly not the cleanest output, but setting a few options would fix that. The first of them is called:

```
.mode column
```

and this would output a neatly spaces resultset rather than the squashed one we saw before (Listing 2-14).

Listing 2-14. Turning on the column mode

```
sqlite> .mode column
sqlite> select * from proglang_tbl;
1           Fortran     Backus      1955
2           Lisp        McCarthy    1958
3           Cobol       Hopper      1959
```

Ah, much better! But there is still a little room for improvement here. We see that column headers are still missing from the output and having them would be advantageous. So we turn on the headers option and the result starts looking pretty neat (Listing 2-15).

Listing 2-15. Turning on the headers in sqlite3

```
sqlite> .headers on
sqlite> select * from proglang_tbl;
id          language    author      year
----------  ----------  ----------  ----------
1           Fortran     Backus      1955
2           Lisp        McCarthy    1958
3           Cobol       Hopper      1959
```

I recommend that you keep these options turned on for your learning sessions. The output becomes much easier to verify at a glance.

CHAPTER 3

The Benefit of Constraints

Relational databases are well into their fourth decade of dominance as a data storage and organization mechanism. A large part of this success is owed to the flexibility of the data model. It is easy to visualize all kinds of data fitting into a neat tabular structure with predefined columns.

The flexibility also extends to querying – while creating and populating tables, little restriction is placed upon what you can query from a table. You might try to generate completely new insights from a table you hadn't thought of before. To enable all of this, relational databases expect a certain amount of discipline and thought being put upfront when designing your tables. Neat tables with well-defined data types are essential for success, and certain rules help you keep on this path of good database design.

A **constraint** is a rule that you apply or abide by while doing SQL operations. They are useful in cases where you wish to make the data inside your database more meaningful and/or structured.

© Rahul Batra 2018
R. Batra, *SQL Primer*, https://doi.org/10.1007/978-1-4842-3576-8_3

The Null Constraint

Consider the example of the programming languages table – every programming language that has been created must have an author (whether a single person, a couple, or committee). Similarly it should have a year when it was introduced, be it the year it first appeared as a research paper or the year a working compiler for it was written. In such cases, it makes sense to create your table in such a way that certain fields do not accept a *NULL* (empty) value.

A null value does not mean 0 (zero) or an empty string like ''. Think of it as either empty or undefined. If you haven't captured someone's age while populating a table, you can't assume their age to be 0. This might have serious implications if someone was using this data for statistical analysis. Putting a null value there makes much more sense.

We now modify our previous CREATE TABLE statement so that we can apply the NULL constraint to some fields (Listing 3-1).

Listing 3-1. Creating a table with NULL constraints

```
CREATE TABLE proglang_tblcopy (
id        INTEGER    NOT NULL,
language  VARCHAR(20) NOT NULL,
author    VARCHAR(25) NOT NULL,
year      INTEGER    NOT NULL,
standard  VARCHAR(10) NULL);
```

In this table, we only allow the *standard* field to have a null value. Every other field ends with the option NOT NULL, which specifies that this field must necessarily have a value. All fields by default are nullable in most database management systems, so you have to specify a non-nullable field. Writing the word NULL to specify a nullable field is optional.

If we try to insert a row into this table with a *NULL* value in one of the non-nullable fields like *year*, we expect an error message to be thrown at us. In both SQLite and PostgreSQL, we represent a null value with the literal null noting the lack of any quotation marks that generally enclose strings (Listings 3-2, 3-3). Null is not a string value and writing 'null' makes an actual string of length 4 and is decidedly non-null. Other database management systems might represent null values in a different way, so check your manual for such details.

Listing 3-2. Inserting a null value in SQLite

```
sqlite> INSERT INTO proglang_tblcopy
VALUES (1, 'Fortran', 'Backus', null, 'ANSI');

Error: NOT NULL constraint failed: proglang_tblcopy.year
```

Listing 3-3. Inserting a null value in PostgreSQL

```
testdb=# INSERT INTO proglang_tblcopy
VALUES (1, 'Fortran', 'Backus', null, 'ANSI');

ERROR:  null value in column "year" violates not-null
constraint
DETAIL:  Failing row contains (1, Fortran, Backus, null, ANSI).
```

We see in this case that we have achieved our objective of creating a table in which the field's *id, language, author,* and *year* cannot be empty for any row, but the new field *standard* can take empty values. We now go about trying to insert new rows into this table using an alternative *INSERT* syntax.

Selective Fields INSERT

From our last encounter with the INSERT statement, we saw that we had to specify the data to be inserted in the same order as specified during the creation of the table in question. We now look at another variation that will allow us to overcome this limitation and handle inserting rows with embedded NULL values in their fields by not specifying them at all (Listing 3-4). While this approach may seem verbose initially, its advantages quickly outweigh any statement length-related concerns.

Listing 3-4. General Syntax of INSERT with selected fields

```
INSERT INTO <Table_Name>

(<Field Name 1>,
 <Field Name 2>,
 . . .
 <Field Name N>)

VALUES

(<Value For Field 1>,
 <Value For Field 2>,
 . . .
 <Value For Field N>);
```

Since we specify the field order in the statement itself, we are free to reorder the values sequence in the same statement, thus removing the first limitation. Also, if we wish to enter an empty (NULL) value in any of the fields for a record, it is easy to do so by simply not including the field's name in the first part of the statement. The statement would run fine without specifying any fields you wish to omit, provided they do not have a NOT NULL constraint attached to them.

We now write some *INSERT* statements for the *proglang_tblcopy* table, in which we try to insert some languages that have not been standardized by any organizations and some which have been (Listing 3-5).

Listing 3-5. Inserting new data into the proglang_tblcopy table

```
INSERT INTO proglang_tblcopy
 (id, language, author, year, standard)
VALUES
 (1, 'Prolog', 'Colmerauer', '1972', 'ISO');

INSERT INTO proglang_tblcopy
 (id, language, author, year)
VALUES
 (2, 'Perl', 'Wall', '1987');

INSERT INTO proglang_tblcopy
 (id, year, standard, language, author)
VALUES
 (3, '1964', 'ANSI', 'APL', 'Iverson');
```

When you run this through your SQL interface, three new rows would be inserted into the table. Notice the ordering of the third row; it is not the same sequence we used to create the table. Also, since Perl (row id 2) has not been standardized by an international body yet, so we do not specify the field name itself while doing the INSERT operation. This ensures that the *standard* field for the row is populated with null.

To verify the results of these statements (Table 3-1) and to make sure that the correct data went into the correct fields, we run a simple query as before.

```
SELECT * FROM proglang_tblcopy;
```

Table 3-1. *Result of the Query Run on proglang_tblcopy*

id	language	author	year	standard
1	Prolog	Colmerauer	1972	ISO
2	Perl	Wall	1987	
3	APL	Iverson	1964	ANSI

Nulls are often shown by SQL interfaces by a blank space or a question mark (?) or sometimes even the word 'null' or '(null)'. Each implementation is free to choose its representation since it is not standardized among vendors.

Check Constraints

Data must be meaningful for someone to derive insights from it. A great advantage of relational databases is that they enable good structuring of data, proper data type-based storage, and null value rules. *Check constraints* go a step even further by providing validation of what values are allowed in a particular field.

They allow you to provide a logical expression against which inserted values are tested and subsequently accepted or rejected. For example, suppose we wish to ensure that in our programming languages table, no language creation year could be less than or equal to 1950 (Listing 3-6). This would stop someone from entering values like 190 for the year, which makes sense unless we wish to capture programming languages created during the Roman Empire!

Listing 3-6. Creating a check constraint for the year field

```
CREATE TABLE proglang_constraints (
id        INTEGER     NOT NULL,
language  VARCHAR(20) NOT NULL,
author    VARCHAR(25) NOT NULL,
year      INTEGER     NOT NULL
CHECK (year > 1950),
standard  VARCHAR(10) NULL);
```

Note the full definition of the *year* field that defines the check constraint after the NOT NULL constraint. The logical expression we are testing against is year > 1950, which disallows any row containing a year value less than 1951. Let's try entering such a row to test the hypotheses (Listing 3-7).

Listing 3-7. Trying to violate a check constraint

```
testdb=# INSERT INTO proglang_constraints
        (id, language, author, year)
        VALUES
        (1, 'Short Code', 'Mauchly', 1949);

ERROR:  new row for relation "proglang_constraints" violates
check constraint "proglang_constraints_year_check"

DETAIL:  Failing row contains (1, Short Code, Mauchly, 1949,
null).
```

While an underused feature, check constraints are extremely useful. A lot of application software code is written with the purpose of validating data to be inserted, an area where check constraints can help immensely.

Primary Key Constraint

The mathematical concept behind the relational data model was Set theory. This area of discrete maths deals with unordered bag of values that can be uniquely identified, that is, contains no duplicates. For a table, a value is a record of data and a key column for each record is the perfect way to identify it.

A *primary key* is used to make each record unique in at least one way by forcing a field to have a unique value. They do not have to be restricted to only one field; a combination of them can also be defined as a primary key for a table. One must think carefully about the logical implications of choosing a field or a combination of them as a primary key.

Often the best primary key candidates are not our instinctive identifiers for a collection. If you were storing data about people, their names are something we identify them with in real-life scenarios. But what would happen in the unforgiving world of primary keys if two people were named 'David Childs'?

In our programming languages table, the *id* field is a good choice for applying the primary key constraint. We will now modify our CREATE TABLE statement to incorporate this (Listing 3-8).

Listing 3-8. A CREATE TABLE statement with a primary key

```
CREATE TABLE proglang_tbltmp (
id        INTEGER     NOT NULL  PRIMARY KEY,
language  VARCHAR(20) NOT NULL,
author    VARCHAR(25) NOT NULL,
year      INTEGER     NOT NULL,
standard  VARCHAR(10) NULL);
```

ID fields are usually chosen as primary fields. Note that in this particular table, the *language* field would have also worked, since a language name is unique. However, if we have a table that describes people, we should try to find a logically unique field like their SSN number or employee ID number.

Even though the concept of a primary key seems to be natural and necessary, most database implementations don't really enforce it. This includes the two databases used for examples in this book – *PostgreSQL* and *SQLite*. You are free to create a table without any primary keys (like we did before this section came along) and insert exactly duplicated data again and again. Not an ideal scenario but allowed nonetheless if you are so inclined.

Let us add some duplicated rows in our *proglang_tblcopy* table that we were working with in the beginning of the chapter (Listing 3-9).

Listing 3-9. Inserting duplicate data in a table without a primary key

```
INSERT INTO proglang_tblcopy
 (id, language, author, year)
VALUES
 (2, 'Perl', 'Wall', '1987');

INSERT INTO proglang_tblcopy
 (id, language, author, year)
VALUES
 (2, 'Perl', 'Wall', '1987');
```

Note that we already had three unique rows in the table to which we added two duplicated ones. The execution of the INSERT statements was silent, indicating success. Let's verify the contents of the table now (Table 3-2).

```
SELECT * FROM proglang_tblcopy;
```

Table 3-2. *Result of the Query Run on proglang_tblcopy Showing Duplicated Rows*

id	language	author	year	standard
1	Prolog	Colmerauer	1972	ISO
2	Perl	Wall	1987	
3	APL	Iverson	1964	ANSI
2	Perl	Wall	1987	
2	Perl	Wall	1987	

If we try to add duplicate records in our table containing the primary key constraint – *proglang_tbltmp*, we promptly get an error thrown at us (Listing 3-10).

Listing 3-10. Trying to add a duplicate record violating a primary key constraint

```
INSERT INTO proglang_tbltmp
 (id, language, author, year)
VALUES
 (2, 'Perl', 'Wall', '1987');

ERROR:  duplicate key value violates unique constraint
"proglang_tbltmp_pkey"
DETAIL:  Key (id)=(2) already exists.
```

Unique Key Constraints

A *unique key* like a primary key is also used to make each record inside a table unique. Once you have defined the primary key of a table, any other fields you wish to enforce as unique is done through this constraint. Well thought-out uniqueness constraints go a long way in ensuring that the data inside the table is sane.

For example, in our database it now makes sense to have a unique key constraint on the *language* field (Listing 3-11). This would ensure none of the records would duplicate information about the same programming language even if the *id* field was non-matching.

Listing 3-11. Programming languages table with the unique key constraint

```
CREATE TABLE proglang_tbluk (
id        INTEGER     NOT NULL  PRIMARY KEY,
language  VARCHAR(20) NOT NULL  UNIQUE,
author    VARCHAR(25) NOT NULL,
year      INTEGER     NOT NULL,
standard  VARCHAR(10) NULL);
```

We will now try to insert two rows about the language *Prolog* cleverly changing the *id* field to test out our unique constraint (Listing 3-12).

Listing 3-12. Inserting duplicate data in a table with a unique key constraint

```
testdb=# INSERT INTO proglang_tbluk
 (id, language, author, year, standard)
VALUES
 (1, 'Prolog', 'Colmerauer', 1972, 'ISO');

INSERT 0 1

testdb=# INSERT INTO proglang_tbluk
 (id, language, author, year, standard)
VALUES
 (2, 'Prolog', 'Colmerauer', 1972, 'ISO');

ERROR:  duplicate key value violates unique constraint
"proglang_tbluk_language_key"
DETAIL:  Key (language)=(Prolog) already exists.
```

Note that we write the word UNIQUE in front of the field and omit the KEY in the table creation command. You can have as many fields with unique constraints as you wish.

We will revisit the unique and primary key constraints again in Chapter 15 when we discuss indexing.

Differences Between a Primary Key and a Unique Key

You might have noticed that the two constraints discussed above are similar in their purpose. However, there are a couple of differences between them.

1. A primary key field cannot take on a NULL value, whereas a field with a unique constraint can. However, there can be only one such record since each value must be unique due to the very definition of the constraint.

2. You are allowed to define only one primary key constraint for a table, but you can apply the unique constraint to as many fields as you like.

This is a favorite interview question for any job that deals with SQL as far as my experience goes. It is not too unfair considering the importance of these constraints to a logical data model. Just remember to think of a primary key as a NOT NULL UNIQUE constraint.

A primary key ensures a logical way to differentiate between rows of a table. It is the bare minimum criterion for a differentiated record. Unique constraints are usually added as additional rules to ensure data sanity while keeping the business or domain rules in mind. It's not necessary to have them, but they act as gatekeepers to allow only good data through.

CHAPTER 4

Operations on Tables

Tables are the fundamental storage containers of the relational world. A database will typically contain many tables, each representing a collection of entities. As requirements evolve, so do the tables within a database and database administrators (DBA's) routinely perform administrative operations on individual tables like deleting them or changing their definition. While typical database users are not granted permissions to perform such operations on large production databases, nonetheless it is important to be familiar with them for didactic purposes.

You might have noticed that we keep on making new tables whenever we are introducing a new concept. This has had the not-so-desirable effect of populating our database with many similar tables each holding programming languages data but with slightly varying definitions and constraints. We will now go about dropping unneeded tables and modifying existing ones to suit our needs.

Dropping Tables

The deletion of tables in SQL is achieved through the DROP TABLE command. DROP is actually a top-level SQL command, much like CREATE, which performs a deletion operation on many kinds of database objects. To delete a table, we simply append it with the database object type – a TABLE in this case.

© Rahul Batra 2018
R. Batra, *SQL Primer*, https://doi.org/10.1007/978-1-4842-3576-8_4

We will now drop any superfluous tables we have created during the previous lessons (Listing 4-1). Note that dropping a table means deleting a table and any data inside it without a chance of recovery. So be careful while writing DROP commands.

Listing 4-1. Dropping the temporary tables we created

```
DROP TABLE proglang_tbl;

DROP TABLE proglang_tblcopy;

DROP TABLE proglang_constraints;

DROP TABLE proglang_tbltmp;
```

If you get no errors returned, it means that the tables have been deleted. DROP TABLE only supports dropping a single table at a time conventionally though there are clever ways to go about deleting multiple tables with a single statement.

To verify whether the tables have actually been dropped you have two choices. A simplistic one is to write any query for the table, and you would get an error back similar to Error: no such table: proglang_tbl. The other way is to get the listing of currently existing tables from the database *catalog*, which is a database that the DBMS internally uses to keep a track of databases, tables, and other objects that users create. Querying the catalog in SQLite for a listing of tables is extremely simple (Listing 4-2).

Listing 4-2. Listing existing tables in SQLite

```
sqlite> .tables
proglang_tbluk
```

Doing the same thing in PostgreSQL is slightly longer, but it is a SELECT query on the catalog database (Listing 4-3).

Listing 4-3. Listing existing tables in PostgreSQL

```
testdb=# SELECT table_name
         FROM information_schema.tables
         WHERE table_schema = 'public'
         AND table_type = 'BASE TABLE';

    table_name
----------------------
 proglang_tbluk
(1 row)
```

If the query seems complicated to you, it is because it contains parts
and syntax that we have not covered yet. But rest assured, the syntax
will start making perfect sense by the end of the chapter on queries.
For now we can infer that the table data in PostgreSQL is stored in the
`information_schema.tables` catalog table.

Creating New Tables from Existing Tables

You might have noticed that we have dropped the *proglang_tbl* table,
and we now have with us only the *proglang_tbluk* table that has all the
necessary constraints and fields. The latter's name was chosen when
we were discussing the unique key constraint, but it now seems logical
to migrate this table structure (and any corresponding data) back to the
name *proglang_tbl*. We achieve this by creating a copy of the table using
a combination of both CREATE TABLE and SELECT commands and learn
a new clause in the process – AS (Listing 4-4). This combination has a
particularly catchy name – *CTAS* and was introduced in the SQL:2003
standard but not all DBMS systems implement it yet, notably Microsoft
SQL Server.

Listing 4-4. General syntax for creating a new table from an existing one

```
CREATE TABLE <New Table>
 AS
SELECT <Selection> FROM <Old Table>;
```

Since our *proglang_tbluk* contains only one record, we will push some more sample data in it so that we can later verify whether the records themselves got copied or not. Notice that we give the field names explicitly, or else the second row (which contains no *standard* field value) would give an error similar to:

```
sqlite> INSERT INTO proglang_tbluk
        VALUES
        (2, 'Perl', 'Wall', 1987);

Error: table proglang_tbluk has 5 columns but 4 values were
supplied
```

in SQLite. A lot of other DBMS's like *Ingres* would also not accept such a cavalier approach to inserting data. PostgreSQL, however, would accept such a statement provided it could unambiguously insert the data that in this case it can due to the omitted value being the last nullable field only. I would advise writing the column names explicitly wherever possible. We will follow this sage advice in Listing 4-5.

Listing 4-5. Inserting some more data into the proglang_tbluk table

```
INSERT INTO proglang_tbluk (id, language, author, year)
VALUES (2, 'Perl', 'Wall', '1987');

INSERT INTO proglang_tbluk (id, year, standard, language, author)
VALUES (3, '1964', 'ANSI', 'APL', 'Iverson');
```

To create an exact copy of the existing table, we use the same selection criteria as we have seen before - * (star). This will select all the fields from the existing table and create the new table with them along with any records (Listing 4-6). It is possible to use only a subset of fields from the old table by modifying the selection criteria and we will see this later.

Listing 4-6. Re-creating a new table from an existing one

```
CREATE TABLE proglang_tbl
 AS
SELECT * FROM proglang_tbluk;
```

If you are using *psql*, you would see the prompt displaying SELECT 3, which gives an indicator of how many rows were selected and inserted into the new table. We now run a simple SELECT query to see whether our objective was achieved or not (Table 4-1).

```
SELECT * FROM proglang_tbl;
```

Table 4-1. *Result of the Query Run on proglang_tbl*

id	language	author	year	standard
1	Prolog	Colmerauer	1972	ISO
2	Perl	Wall	1987	
3	APL	Iverson	1964	ANSI

The two tables are now exactly identical but are not linked to each other in any way. If you drop any of the tables, the other one will not be affected. Similarly, inserting new data in one of them will not insert the data in the other one from now on.

Modifying Tables

After a table has been created, you can still modify its structure using the
ALTER TABLE command (Listing 4-7). What we mean by modify is that
you can change field types, sizes, even add or delete columns. Not all
database management systems support all operations of ALTER TABLE. To
get around such limitations, people frequently copy the data over to a new
table that has the newly required structure. While altering a table is not an
SQL command you'd use very often (hopefully!), you should be familiar
with it.

There are some rules you have to abide by while altering a table and
these are usually spelled out in detail by your particular DBMS manual.
For now, we will see a simple example to modify the field *author* for the
proglang_tbl table.

Listing 4-7. General syntax of a simple ALTER TABLE command

```
ALTER TABLE <Table name> <Operation> <Field with clauses>;
```

To keep our *proglang_tbl* intact, we are going to be making our changes
to the old *proglang_tbluk* table. We want to make the *author* field hold
a tad bit more maximum data length of 30 characters instead of 25. The
operation to choose in this case is ALTER COLUMN, which would modify our
existing field (Listing 4-8).

Listing 4-8. Altering the author field

```
ALTER TABLE proglang_tbluk
 ALTER COLUMN author TYPE varchar(30);
```

If you not using SQLite, the above query should execute quietly in
PostgreSQL. SQLite unfortunately does not support altering a column
size but happily supports addition of new columns. So let's add another
requirement of adding a nullable column *current_status* to our table fields
(Listing 4-9).

Listing 4-9. Adding a new current_status field

```
ALTER TABLE proglang_tbluk
 ADD COLUMN current_status VARCHAR(32) NULL;
```

We have used the ADD COLUMN operation in this case for the ALTER TABLE command. Unsurprisingly we hope to add this new 32-character length column to our *proglang_tbluk* with this statement.

The many faces of ALTER TABLE   Altering a table is one of those commands where even after three decades, there are discrepancies. For example, you already saw that the ALTER COLUMN doesn't work in SQLite. *Ingres*; another, DBMS, expects you to write ALTER only, which coincidentally also works fine for PostgreSQL. We choose the former to be explicit. *Oracle* on the other hand has gone a completely different way, and it uses MODIFY instead of ALTER COLUMN.

Similarly, while adding a column, you could write only ADD <column name> in PostgreSQL or SQLite and expect it to work.

However, while altering data types, PostgreSQL expects you to write TYPE between the column name and the new data type specification whereas Ingres wouldn't expect it.

Always keep the manual of your DBMS handy!

Showing Table Information in PostgreSQL

If you are thinking about using the database system catalog to get table definition information to verify your ALTER TABLE results, congratulations! You are indeed correct in thinking that. As before, the query might seem a little more than we can handle correctly at this point in the text, but it's output is highly readable (Listing 4-10).

Listing 4-10. Viewing field information in PostgreSQL by querying the catalog

```
testdb=# SELECT column_name,
               data_type,
               character_maximum_length
        FROM INFORMATION_SCHEMA.COLUMNS
        WHERE table_name = 'proglang_tbluk';

 column_name    |    data_type     | character_maximum_length
----------------+------------------+--------------------------
 id             | integer          |
 language       | character varying |                      20
 author         | character varying |                      30
 year           | integer          |
 standard       | character varying |                      10
 current_status | character varying |                      32
(6 rows)
```

Both our changes to the fields *author* and *current_status* seem to be reflected correctly. There are a few other databases where such a query would work, but unfortunately this is another area where a lot of DBMS implementations differ widely.

A PostgreSQL *psql*-specific method is to use \d+ <table name>, which gives almost the same information along with some other values by default (Listing 4-11). I personally prefer the Listing 4-10 version that queries the catalog.

Listing 4-11. Describing the schema of the table in psql

```
testdb=# \d+ proglang_tbluk;
                        Table "public.proglang_tbluk"
     Column     |          Type          | Modifiers | Storage  |
----------------+------------------------+-----------+----------+
 id             | integer                |           | plain    |
 language       | character varying(20)  |           | extended |
 author         | character varying(30)  |           | extended |
 year           | integer                |           | plain    |
 standard       | character varying(10)  |           | extended |
 current_status | character varying(32)  |           | extended |
Indexes:
    "proglang_tbluk_pkey" PRIMARY KEY, btree (id)
    "proglang_tbluk_language_key" UNIQUE CONSTRAINT,
    btree (language)
```

Showing Table Information in SQLite

As we have already discussed SQLite, as of the writing of this text, does not support modification to column sizes in a table using ALTER TABLE. It does however allow you to add a new column, and we added the *current_status* field like with PostgreSQL. Let's now verify this by looking at the table information inside the SQLite shell.

SQLite has its own special *dot syntax* commands that allow certain useful database management tasks. We have already seen the .open command used to create and open a database and .tables to list the table names. Similarly we can use the .schema command to get table information (Listing 4-12).

45

Listing 4-12. Displaying schema information in SQLite

```
sqlite> .schema proglang_tbluk

CREATE TABLE proglang_tbluk (
id              INTEGER     NOT NULL  PRIMARY KEY,
language        VARCHAR(20) NOT NULL  UNIQUE,
author          VARCHAR(25) NOT NULL,
year            INTEGER     NOT NULL,
standard        VARCHAR(10) NULL,
current_status VARCHAR(32) NULL);
```

Notice how the new column is added at the end while the length of the *author* field remains 25 characters.

Showing Table Information in Other DBMS's

If you are not practicing on either of the DBMS implementations mentioned above, there might be other ways to verify table field-level information. For example, Ingres utilizes the HELP TABLE <table name> command, which can be run on its *isql* shell.

A lot of other DBMS's like Oracle use the DESCRIBE command to view a table definition. While the information this command shows may vary from one DBMS to another, they at least show the field name, its data type, and whether or not NULL values are allowed for the particular field. The general syntax of the command is given below (Listing 4-13).

Listing 4-13. The general syntax of the DESCRIBE statement

```
DESCRIBE <table name>;
```

CHAPTER 5

Writing Basic Queries

A *query* is an SQL statement that is used to extract a subset of data from your database and presents it in a readable format. As we have seen previously, the SELECT command is used to run queries in SQL. You can further add clauses to your query to get a filtered, more meaningful result. The level of flexibility afforded by SQL is one of the reasons it has succeeded as a query language. While there is an entire gamut of add-ons to SELECT, in this chapter we will focus on only two – ORDER BY and WHERE.

Database administration tasks for a well thought-out schema are few and far between, but retrieving meaningful results using queries is something everyone does routinely. Since the majority of operations on a database involve queries, it is important to understand them in detail. While this chapter will only deal with queries run on a single table, you can run a SELECT operation on multiple tables in a single statement.

Selecting a Limited Number of Columns

The intention since the beginning of SQL was to provide an easy-to-use query system to everyday users. They should not have to reach for a programming language to make their report readable. A major facility for this is the ability to display a finite set of columns in the output rather than all the fields of a table.

© Rahul Batra 2018
R. Batra, *SQL Primer*, https://doi.org/10.1007/978-1-4842-3576-8_5

We have already seen how to extract all the data from a table when we were verifying our results in the previous chapters. But as you might have noted in some of our catalog queries – we can extract a subset of data too. We first test this by limiting the number of fields to show in the query output by not specifying the * selection criteria, but by naming the fields explicitly as a comma-separated list (Listing 5-1).

Listing 5-1. Selecting a subset of fields from a table

```
SELECT language,
       year FROM proglang_tbl;
```

language	year
Prolog	1972
Perl	1987
APL	1964

You can see that the query we constructed mentioned the fields we wish to see, that is, *language* and *year*. Also note that the result of this query is useful by itself as a report for looking at the chronology of programming language creation. While this is not a rule enforced by SQL or a relation database management system, it makes sense to construct your query in such a way that the meaning is self-evident if the output is meant to be read by a human. This is the reason we left out the field *id* in the query, since it has no inherent meaning to the reader except if they wish to know the sequential order of the storage of records in the table.

You are free to decide the ordering of the fields in your output. The positioning of a field in a CREATE TABLE statement has no effect on any SELECT query you run on it. Indeed, you are even free to duplicate a field as many times as you wish in your output. Whether it makes sense to do so is debatable! But as long as the field names in the comma-separated list to SELECT is valid, it will show up in the output.

Ordering the Results

You might have noticed that in our previous query output, the languages were printed out in the same order as we had inserted them. But what if we wanted to sort the results by the year the language was created in. The chronological order might make more sense if we wish to view the development of programming languages through the decades. In such cases, we take the help of the ORDER BY clause. To achieve our purpose, we modify our query with this additional clause (Listing 5-2).

Listing 5-2. Usage of the ORDER BY clause

```
SELECT language,
       year
FROM proglang_tbl ORDER BY year;
```

language	year
APL	1964
Prolog	1972
Perl	1987

The astute reader will notice that the output of our ORDER BY clause was ascending. This is the default ordering that can be made explicit by appending the argument ASC to the column we wish to sort. To reverse this, we use the argument DESC to our ORDER BY clause as below (Listing 5-3).

Listing 5-3. Usage of the ORDER BY clause with the DESC argument

```
SELECT language,
       year
FROM proglang_tbl ORDER BY year DESC;
```

language	year
Perl	1987
Prolog	1972
APL	1964

Ordering is not limited to numeric fields. You can order character-based columns too. The sorting method is alphabetical starting with the first character and subsequently moving to the next sequential characters if the character is the same. Let us try ordering our query result by the *language* field this time (Listing 5-4).

Listing 5-4. Usage of the ORDER BY clause with a character based column

```
SELECT language,
       year
FROM proglang_tbl ORDER BY language;
```

language	year
APL	1964
Perl	1987
Prolog	1972

Ordering Using Field Abbreviations

A useful shortcut in SQL involves ordering a query result using an integer abbreviation instead of the complete field name. The abbreviations are formed starting with 1, which is given to the first field specified in the query; 2 to the second field; and so on. Let's rewrite our query to sort the output by descending year using field abbreviations (Listing 5-5).

Listing 5-5. Ordered SELECT query in descending order using field abbreviations

```
SELECT language,
       year
FROM proglang_tbl ORDER BY 2 DESC;
```

language	year
Perl	1987
Prolog	1972
APL	1964

The 2 argument given to the ORDER BY clause signifies ordering by the second field specified in the query, namely *year*. Over time I have realized that the best use of field abbreviations is while you are querying a database system interactively. Rarely is it a good idea to use field abbreviations if you are embedding SQL inside a programming language.

Ordering by Multiple Columns

What if you wanted to order your results by more than one column? It would be a plausible scenario where some of the values of the ordering column are the same. For example, supposing you had a table having student grades and names. You want to order the students by their grades, but a lot of students have gotten the Grade A. So you apply a second ordering by name, sorting alphabetically all grade A students, then grade B students and so on.

Let's try to see a working example of this using our programming languages table. But for that we need to insert a few more rows in there (Listing 5-6).

Listing 5-6. Inserting a few more languages in our table

```
INSERT INTO proglang_tbl
 (id, language, author, year, standard)
VALUES
 (4, 'JOVIAL', 'Schwartz', 1959, 'US-DOD');

INSERT INTO proglang_tbl
 (id, language, author, year, standard)
VALUES
 (5, 'APT', 'Ross', 1959, 'ISO');
```

Now let us order our programming languages table by *year* and *language* keeping in mind that our newly inserted languages have the same year of creation (Listing 5-7).

Listing 5-7. Ordering by more than one columns

```
SELECT language,
       year
FROM proglang_tbl ORDER BY year, language;
```

language	year
APT	1959
JOVIAL	1959
APL	1964
Prolog	1972
Perl	1987

You can even use different ordering types for each of the columns (Listing 5-8).

Listing 5-8. Combining different ordering types

```
SELECT language,
       year
FROM proglang_tbl
ORDER BY year DESC, language ASC;
```

language	year
Perl	1987
Prolog	1972
APL	1964
APT	1959
JOVIAL	1959

Notice how *APT* came before *JOVIAL* because we had mentioned an ascending order for the *language* field.

Putting Conditions with WHERE

We have already seen how to select a subset of data available in a table by limiting the fields queried. We will now limit the number of records retrieved in a query using conditions. The WHERE clause is used to achieve this, and it can be combined with explicit field selection or ordering clauses to provide meaningful output.

For a query to run successfully and fetch data from a table, it must have at least two parts – the SELECT and the FROM clause.[1] After this we place the optional WHERE condition and then the ordering clause. Thus, if we wanted to see the programming language (and its author), which was standardized by ANSI, we'd write our query as below (Listing 5-9).

---

[1]If we let go of our from a table requirement, we can write a query with just SELECT. Try SELECT 1 in your DBMS and see the output.

53

Listing 5-9. Using a WHERE conditional

```
SELECT language,
       author
FROM proglang_tbl
WHERE standard = 'ANSI';
```

language	author
APL	Iverson

As you may have noticed, the query we formulated specified the *language* and *author* fields, but the condition was imposed on a separate field altogether – *standard*. Thus we can safely say that while we can choose what columns to display, our conditionals can work on a record with any of its fields.

You are by no means restricted to use = (equals) for your conditions. It is perfectly acceptable to choose other operators like < and >. You can also include the ORDER BY clause and sort your output. An example is given below (Listing 5-10).

Listing 5-10. Combining the WHERE and ORDER BY

```
SELECT language,
       author,
       year
FROM proglang_tbl
WHERE year > 1970
ORDER BY author;
```

language	author	year
Prolog	Colmerauer	1972
Perl	Wall	1987

Notice that the output only shows programming languages developed after 1970 (at least according to our database). Also since the ordering is done by a varchar field, the sorting is done alphabetically in an ascending order.

Combining Conditions

If we can only specify one condition using the WHERE clause, it will fulfill only a tiny fraction of real-world requirements. We can however construct complex conditions using the *boolean* operators AND and OR.

When we want our resultset to satisfy all of the multiple conditions, we use the AND operator (Listing 5-11).

Listing 5-11. Using the AND operator to combine conditions

```
SELECT language,
       author,
       year
FROM proglang_tbl
WHERE year > 1970 AND standard IS NULL;
```

language	author	year
Perl	Wall	1987

We have now combined the two conditions, meaning any row in the resultset must satisfy both the criteria mentioned. In our case, there is only one such row – *Perl*.

An interesting point to note is our construction of the second conditional. We specify that the *standard* field should be a null value by specifying IS NULL. This is not the same as saying standard = NULL. If we attempt to write the latter as our conditional, we would get an empty result.

While this may seem counterintuitive, it actually makes perfect sense. A null is supposed to signify undefined values, not a precise value like infinity or 0 or even a complex number. We cannot rationalize the precise equivalence operator = for a null, and thus SQL interpreters use the IS NULL comparison.

If we want our resultset to satisfy any one of our conditions, we use the OR operator. Let's use this operator in the above example but with a different intention. We want all languages that were either created after 1970 *or* don't have a standardizing body (Listing 5-12).

Listing 5-12. Using the OR operator

```
SELECT language,
       author,
       year
FROM proglang_tbl
WHERE year > 1970 OR standard IS NULL;
```

language	author	year
Prolog	Colmerauer	1972
Perl	Wall	1987

Prolog only satisfies the first criterion that it was created after 1970 but was actually standardized by ISO. *Perl* satisfies both criteria and is also rightly shown. If we had a language in our table without a standardizing body but created before 1970, it would also sneak up on the resultset here.

We can even create yet more complex queries by combining the AND and OR operators. One has to be careful to not make the logic of the filtering using these operators complex or unreadable.

CHAPTER 6

Manipulating Data

In this chapter we study the *Data Manipulation Language (DML)* part of SQL that is used to make changes to the data inside a relational database. The three basic commands of DML are as follows.

- **INSERT** Populates tables with new data

- **UPDATE** Updates existing data

- **DELETE** Deletes data from tables

We have already seen a few examples on the INSERT statement including simple inserts, selective field insertions, and null value inserts. Thus we will concentrate on other ways to use this statement.

Inserting Data into a Table from Another Table

You can insert new records into a table from another one by using a combination of INSERT and SELECT. This is pretty close to the way we combined CREATE TABLE and SELECT to create a new table with rows from another table.

Since a query would return you some records, combining it with an insertion command would enter these records into the new table. You can even use a WHERE conditional to limit or filter the records you wish to enter into the new table. We will now create a new table called *stdlang_tbl*, which

© Rahul Batra 2018
R. Batra, *SQL Primer*, https://doi.org/10.1007/978-1-4842-3576-8_6

will have only two fields – *language* and *standard*. In this we would insert rows from the *proglang_tbl* table that have a non-null value in the *standard* field (Listing 6-1). This will also demonstrate our first use of a boolean operator – NOT.

Listing 6-1. Using INSERT and SELECT to conditionally load data into another table

```
CREATE TABLE stdlang_tbl
 (language varchar(20),
  standard varchar (10));

INSERT INTO stdlang_tbl
 SELECT language,
        standard
 FROM proglang_tbl
 WHERE standard IS NOT NULL;
```

Note that we had to create the table separately in this case and then insert data into it using INSERT and SELECT. The NOT inverts the IS NULL test, that is, if something is a null value instead of normally returning a *true*, the NOT makes the conditional return a *false*.

NOT, NULL, True and False   If we consider boolean logic principles, the closest analogue to NULL is the value *false*. However NOT inverts a boolean value: *true* becomes *false*, and *false* becomes *true*.

Testing a value with IS NULL is an SQL comparison, returning a *true* for every null value. This is what we have inverted in the example above using NOT. Don't confuse the meaning of this comparison with what boolean value a NULL closely represents.

When you view the contents of this table, you will notice that it has picked up the languages that actually had a *standard* column value (Table 6-1).

Table 6-1. *Contents of Our Newly Created stdlang_tbl table*

language	standard
Prolog	ISO
APL	ANSI
JOVIAL	US-DOD
APT	ISO

The data being populated by INSERT INTO and SELECT must adhere to the constraints defined during table creation. If our *stdlang_tbl* had defined language as its primary key, our insert statements would run fine unless we encountered a duplicate language value (Listing 6-2). This is not a problem in our case currently since the languages are themselves unique.

Listing 6-2. An altered definition of stdlang_tbl with the primary key

```
DROP TABLE stdlang_tbl;

CREATE TABLE stdlang_tbl
 (language varchar(20) PRIMARY KEY,
  standard varchar (10));

INSERT INTO stdlang_tbl
 SELECT language,
        standard
 FROM proglang_tbl
 WHERE standard IS NOT NULL;
```

What would happen if we somehow violated the constraints? For example, let us go about creating a new table *standardizing_bodies* that contains only one field – *name*. The only constraint on this is UNIQUE. We already know that both Prolog and APT from our *proglang_tbl* were standardized by ISO. Let's try to simulate this using code (Listing 6-3).

Listing 6-3. Violating the UNIQUE constraint while INSERT INTO ... SELECT

```
CREATE TABLE standardizing_bodies
 ( name varchar(10) UNIQUE );

INSERT INTO standardizing_bodies
 SELECT standard FROM proglang_tbl
 WHERE standard IS NOT NULL;

ERROR:  duplicate key value violates unique constraint
"standardizing_bodies_name_key"
DETAIL:  Key (name)=(ISO) already exists.
```

Note that the contents of this new table *standardizing_bodies* will be empty. Our INSERT operation was a single statement, not a collection of unique inserts. Thus when the constraint was violated, no data was inserted.

Updating Existing Data

To modify some data in a record, we use the UPDATE command. While it cannot add or delete records (those responsibilities are delegated to other commands), if a record exists it can modify its data even affecting multiple fields in one go and applying conditions. The general syntax of an UPDATE statement is given below (Listing 6-4).

Listing 6-4. General syntax of the UPDATE command

```
UPDATE <table_name> SET
 <column1> = <value>,
 <column2> = <value>,
 <column3> = <value>

 . . .
WHERE <condition>;
```

Let us now return to our *proglang_tbl* table and add a new row about the *Forth* and *Tcl* programming languages (Listing 6-5).

Listing 6-5. Populating some more data in our programming languages table

```
INSERT INTO proglang_tbl
 (id, language, author, year, standard)
VALUES
 (6, 'Forth', 'Moore', 1973, NULL);

INSERT INTO proglang_tbl
 (id, language, author, year, standard)
VALUES
 (7, 'Tcl', 'Ousterhout', 1988, NULL);
```

What if we suddenly wanted to add 10 years to each language's creation year? Since we want to apply the UPDATE logic to every row, we can forego the search conditions (Listing 6-6).

Listing 6-6. Running an UPDATE on all rows of a table

```
UPDATE proglang_tbl SET
 year = year + 10;
```

This query would increase all language creation years by 10. There is no ambiguity here, since the right-hand side year + 10 is calculated first and then assigned to the *year* field. This happens for all rows. To get back to our original dates, simply run the same query with the SET column as year = year – 10.

We later realize that the Forth language was created near 1972 (instead of 1973), and it actually has been standardized in 1994 by the ANSI. Thus we now go about correcting our mistakes by writing our update queries to reflect this data (Listing 6-7). We should note that we must include a search condition for the Forth language only.

Listing 6-7. Updating the Forth language details

```
UPDATE proglang_tbl SET
 year = 1972
WHERE language = 'Forth';

UPDATE proglang_tbl SET
 standard = 'ANSI'
WHERE language = 'Forth';
```

We could have easily combined updating the multiple fields in a single statement, thus saving the DBMS engine the trouble to find the row again (Listing 6-8).

Listing 6-8. Updating multiple fields in a single statement

```
UPDATE proglang_tbl SET
 year = 1972,
 standard = 'ANSI'
WHERE language = 'Forth';
```

If you've typed the statement correctly and no errors are thrown back, the contents of the record in question would have been modified as intended. Verifying the result of the same involves a simple query the likes of which we have seen in previous examples.

Deleting Data from Tables

You can use the DELETE command to delete records from a table. This means that you can choose which records you want to delete based on a condition or delete all records, but you cannot delete certain fields of a record using this statement. The general syntax of the DELETE statement is given below (Listing 6-9).

Listing 6-9. General syntax of DELETE

```
DELETE FROM <table_name>
WHERE <condition>;
```

While putting a conditional clause in the DELETE is optional, it is almost always used – simply because not using it would cause all the records to be deleted from a table, which is a rarely valid need. Luckily, we have a spare table *stdlang_tbl* that is not needed anymore, so let's try deleting all rows from it (Listing 6-10).

Listing 6-10. Deleting all records from a table

```
DELETE FROM stdlang_tbl;
```

If we try to verify contents of this table, we'd get no data rows back. Only the column headers would be visible.

language	standard

We now write the full statement to delete the record corresponding to Forth from the table. Again, we will have to include the search condition in the WHERE clause (Listing 6-11, Table 6-2).

Table 6-2. *proglang_tbl contents After the Record Deletion*

id	language	author	year	standard
1	Prolog	Colmerauer	1972	ISO
2	Perl	Wall	1987	
3	APL	Iverson	1964	ANSI
4	JOVIAL	Schwartz	1959	US-DOD
5	APT	Ross	1959	ISO
7	Tcl	Ousterhout	1988	

Listing 6-11. Deleting a record from the proglang_tbl table

```
DELETE FROM proglang_tbl WHERE language = 'Forth';
```

You should always be careful about the WHERE clauses you put on a DELETE statement. They should never be too broad, lest you end up deleting more data than you intended.

CHAPTER 7

Organizing Your Data

Since this is a text meant to teach SQL to people unfamiliar with it, our data has been very simplistic. The number of fields you'd wish to store in your database would be a larger value than the five-column table we saw in earlier chapters. Also, some assumptions were made intrinsically on the kind of data we will store in the table. But this is not always the case in real life.

In reality the data we encounter will be complex, even redundant. This is where the study of data modeling techniques and database design come in. While it is advised that the reader refer to a more comprehensive treatise on this subject, nonetheless we will try to study some good relational database design principles since the study would come in handy while learning SQL statements for multiple tables.

Normalization

Let us suppose we have a database of employees in a fictional institution as given below (Table 7-1). If the database structure has not been modeled but has been extracted from a raw collection of information available, *redundancy* is expected.

© Rahul Batra 2018
R. Batra, *SQL Primer*, https://doi.org/10.1007/978-1-4842-3576-8_7

Table 7-1. *The Fictional Firm's Employee Data*

employee_id	name	skill	manager_id	location
1	Socrates	Philosophy	(null)	Greece
2	Plato	Writing	1	Greece
3	Aristotle	Science	2	Greece
4	Descartes	Philosophy	(null)	France
4	Descartes	Philosophy	(null)	Netherlands

We can see that *Descartes* has two rows because he spent his life in both France and Netherlands. Doesn't seem very elegant, does it? Now if at a later point we decide that we wish to classify him with a different skill, we would have to update both his rows since they should contain an identical (primary) skill.

Wouldn't it be saner to have a separate table for skills and somehow allow the records that share the same skill to refer to this table? This way if we wish to reflect that both Socrates and Descartes were thinkers in *Western Philosophy*, renaming the skill record in the second table would do the trick.

This process of breaking down a raw database into logical tables and removing redundancies is called *Normalization*. There are even levels of normalization called *normal forms* that dictate how to achieve the desired design.

There are five accepted normal forms that serious database administrators and developers are familiar with. They range from *first normal form* 1NF to *fifth normal form* 5NF These forms are progressive in nature, meaning that a design in 3NF is also 1NF and 2NF compliant. Since the origin of these forms are based in academic research, the working developers usually restrict themselves to 3NF or 4NF in most cases. Again, we advise the reader refer to a more comprehensive text dealing with database design and normalization. We will do mere lip service in exploring these vast fields.

For now, let's turn to our programming languages data to see the need for normalization playing out.

Atomicity

In the programming language examples that we've seen, our assumption has always been that a language has a single author. But there are countless languages where multiple people contributed to the core design and should rightfully be acknowledged in our table. How would we go about making such a record? Let us take the case of BASIC, which was designed by John Kemeny and Thomas Kurtz. The easiest option to add this new record into the table is to fit both authors in the *author* field (Table 7-2).

Table 7-2. *A Record with a Non-Atomic Field Value*

id	language	author	year	standard
1	Prolog	Colmerauer	1972	ISO
2	Perl	Wall	1987	(null)
3	APL	Iverson	1964	ANSI
4	Tcl	Ousterhout	1988	(null)
5	BASIC	Kemeny, Kurtz	1964	ANSI

You can immediately see that it would be difficult to write a query to retrieve this record based on the *author* field. If the data written as "Kemeny, Kurtz" or "Kurtz, Kemeny" or even "Kemeny & Kurtz," it would be extremely difficult to put the right string in the WHERE conditional clause of the query. After all, it is possible that the person who inserted the data is not the same as the one querying it.

The correct solution is to redesign the table structure to make all field values *atomic*. Atomicity of values means that every intersection of a row and column must contain a single, indivisible value. If in your current design you have some fields containing non-atomic values, you need to start thinking of changing your table structures.

Repeating Groups

Another simple (but ultimately wrong) approach that comes to mind is to split the *author* field into two parts – *author1* and *author2*. If a language has only one author, the *author2* field would contain a null value (Table 7-3). Can you spot the problem that will arise from this design decision?

Table 7-3. *A Table with a Repeating Group*

id	language	author1	author2	year	standard
1	Prolog	Colmerauer	(null)	1972	ISO
2	Perl	Wall	(null)	1987	(null)
3	APL	Iverson	(null)	1964	ANSI
4	Tcl	Ousterhout	(null)	1988	(nul)
5	BASIC	Kemeny	Kurtz	1964	ANSI

This imposes an artificial constraint on how many authors a language can have. It seems to work fine for a couple of them, but what if a programming language was designed by a committee of a dozen or more people, and we did want to include all of them in the credits? At the database design time, how do we fix the number of authors we wish to support?

This kind of design is referred to as a *repeating group* and must be actively avoided. This also has an ugly effect of having too many null values in some of the fields, a first sign of bad database design.

Splitting the Table

Our first stab at table design lumps the languages and authors together. It is natural to think that way because our understanding of the data at first glance views all the fields as a logical whole. All the data to us belongs to the programming languages, the entity being described.

But as we have seen above, the authors of the languages seem to be a distinct entity in our data. We have not even begun to capture multiple languages by the same author, and already we feel a pressing need to distinguish between languages and authors as entities.

The correct design to remove the problems listed above is to *split* the table into two – one holding the author details (Table 7-5) and one detailing the language (Table 7-4).

Table 7-4. *A Table Holding Programming Language Details*

id	language	year	standard
1	Prolog	1972	ISO
2	Perl	1987	(null)
3	APL	1964	ANSI
4	Tcl	1988	(nul)
5	BASIC	1964	ANSI

Table 7-5. *A Table Holding Author Details*

author_id	author	language_id
1	Colmerauer	1
2	Wall	2
3	Ousterhout	4
4	Iverson	3
5	Kemeny	5
6	Kurtz	5

Once you have removed the non-atomicity of fields and repeating groups along with assigning unique id's to your tables, your table structure is now in the *first normal form*. The author table's *language_id* field, which refers to the *id* field of the language table, is called a *foreign key constraint* (Listing 7-1).

Listing 7-1. Creating the new tables

```
CREATE TABLE newlang_tbl
 (id       INTEGER     NOT NULL PRIMARY KEY,
  language VARCHAR(20) NOT NULL,
  year     INTEGER     NOT NULL,
  standard VARCHAR(10) NULL);

CREATE TABLE authors_tbl
 (author_id   INTEGER     NOT NULL,
  author      VARCHAR(25) NOT NULL,
  language_id INTEGER REFERENCES newlang_tbl(id));
```

Notice that in the author's table we've made a foreign key constraint by making the *language_id* field reference the *id* field of the new programming languages table using the keyword REFERENCES. You can only create a foreign key reference as a primary or unique key; otherwise during the constraint creation time we would receive an error similar to the following.

```
ERROR:   there is no unique constraint matching given keys for
referenced table "newlang_tbl"
```

Since we have created a reference to the *language_id*, inserting a row in the author's table that does not yet have a language entry would also result in an error, called a *Referential Integrity* violation (Listing 7-2).

Listing 7-2. A referential integrity violation

```
INSERT INTO authors_tbl
 (author_id, author, language_id)
VALUES
 (5, 'Kemeny', 5)
```

```
ERROR:   insert or update on table "authors_tbl" violates
foreign key constraint "authors_tbl_language_id_fkey"
```

```
DETAIL:   Key (language_id)=(5) is not present in table
"newlang_tbl".
```

However, when done sequentially, that is, the language first and then its corresponding entry in the author table, everything works out (Listing 7-3).

Listing 7-3. Making entries for BASIC in both the tables

```
INSERT INTO newlang_tbl
 (id, language, year, standard)
VALUES
 (5, 'BASIC', 1964, 'ANSI');
```

```
INSERT INTO authors_tbl
 (author_id, author, language_id)
VALUES
 (5, 'Kemeny', 5);
```

Referential Integrity in SQLite   If you tried to run Listing 7-2 in SQLite, you wouldn't get an error back despite there being no *language_id 5* in the *newlang_tbl*. SQLite, by default, turns off referential integrity checking for backward compatibility reasons. To turn it on for your database, run the following pragma in its command shell.

```
PRAGMA foreign_keys = ON;
```

If you now violate referential integrity, we would get a familiar `Error: FOREIGN KEY constraint failed` error message.

Referential integrity is a key benefit of good relational database design. Since it applies to related entities, it ensures that the values of these remain in sync. In our example above, this constraint made sure that we never have an author's data whose created programming language is not captured in the languages table.

When designing databases to solve a business problem, deciding how referential integrity comes into play is a big decision. This is done mainly in discussion with domain experts who understand the business logic of the entities data you are trying to capture.

The other statements to get fully populated tables are given below (Listing 7-4).

Listing 7-4. Fully populating the newly created tables

```
INSERT INTO newlang_tbl
 (id, language, year,  standard)
VALUES
 (1, 'Prolog', 1972, 'ISO');
```

```
INSERT INTO newlang_tbl
 (id, language, year)
VALUES
 (2, 'Perl', 1987);

INSERT INTO newlang_tbl
 (id, language, year,   standard)
VALUES
 (3, 'APL', 1964, 'ANSI');

INSERT INTO newlang_tbl
 (id, language, year)
VALUES
 (4, 'Tcl', 1988);

INSERT INTO authors_tbl
 (author_id, author, language_id)
VALUES (6, 'Kurtz', 5);

INSERT INTO authors_tbl
 (author_id, author, language_id)
VALUES (1, 'Colmerauer', 1);

INSERT INTO authors_tbl
 (author_id, author, language_id)
VALUES (2, 'Wall', 2);

INSERT INTO authors_tbl
 (author_id, author, language_id)
VALUES (3, 'Ousterhout', 4);

INSERT INTO authors_tbl
 (author_id, author, language_id)
VALUES (4, 'Iverson', 3);
```

The Pursuit of Normalization   The man who created the Relational Model and in turn normalization – Dr. Codd – was an academic genius. While he was working at IBM at the time, decidedly non-academia, the whole thing has a whiff of mathematical purity about it.

But the cost of removing redundancies in data is speed. While there may be many advanced levels of normal forms, 1NF-5NF and the lesser-known Boyce-Codd Normal Form, we must not be too pedantic about pursuing the higher normal form. Common sense must prevail in the head of the database designer.

In some cases, denormalization does have the benefit of faster access. Indeed, many in-vogue NoSQL database systems tout redundant data storage as a feature. This obviously comes at the cost of consistency of truth. But then again, when our seemingly random clicks on the Web are captured and analyzed to decide our most suitable insurance provider, perhaps a loss of truth is acceptable.

Nevertheless if 40 years of dominance is anything to go by, unless you have run into a very special case, Codd (and the relational model) is always right.

CHAPTER 8

Doing More with Queries

SQL as a language was created for the end users of the database systems. It just happened to be used by programmers too, but the goal was always a simple, declarative, English-like language to allow anybody familiar with computers and the domain to make sensible reports out of the database system. These reporting capabilities were the direct output of an SQL query, and thus from the very beginning, there have been a lot of options and clauses that can be used with SELECT to make the output more legible.

We have already seen some basic queries, how to order the results of a query, and how to put conditions on the query output. Let us now see more examples of how we can modify our SELECT statements to suit our ever-growing reporting needs.

Counting the Records in a Table

Sometimes we just wish to know how many records exist in a table without actually outputting the entire contents of these records. This can be achieved through the use of an SQL *function* called COUNT. Let us first see the contents of the *proglang_tbl* table when we last left it (Table 8-1).

© Rahul Batra 2018
R. Batra, *SQL Primer*, https://doi.org/10.1007/978-1-4842-3576-8_8

Table 8-1. *proglang_tbl contents from Chapter 6*

id	language	author	year	standard
1	Prolog	Colmerauer	1972	ISO
2	Perl	Wall	1987	
3	APL	Iverson	1964	ANSI
4	JOVIAL	Schwartz	1959	US-DOD
5	APT	Ross	1959	ISO
7	Tcl	Ousterhout	1988	

We can clearly see that using the *id* of the last row of the table, 7 in this case, is clearly not a good idea. While there may have been 7 rows in the table at some point in the past, we had actually deleted the Forth language row. Additionally we cannot always rely on such a field, especially when we could have inserted an *id* of 4711 in the field without anybody complaining. Clearly, we need COUNT to come to our rescue (Listing 8-1).

Listing 8-1. Query to count number of records in the table

```
SELECT COUNT(*) FROM proglang_tbl;
```

The output returned will be a single record with a single field with the value as 6. The function COUNT took one argument, that is, what to count and we provided it with * that means the entire record. Thus we achieved our purpose of counting records in a table.

What would happen if instead of giving an entire record to count, we explicitly specify a column? And what if the column had null values? Let's see this scenario by counting on the *standard* field of the table (Listing 8-2).

Listing 8-2. Query to count number of standard field values in
the table

```
SELECT COUNT(standard) FROM proglang_tbl;
```

If you guessed the output of this query as the value 4, you are correct.
Out of the six rows, two records contain null as their *standard* value leaving
out four languages with a *standard*.

Using DISTINCT with COUNT

The astute reader might have noticed that the number of standardized
languages was computed by counting the number of non-null *standard*
values. However the resultset contained a duplicate standards body
value – *ISO* for both APT and Prolog.

Sometimes it is useful to be able to leave out such duplicates. The
DISTINCT clause allows us to utilize only non-duplicated values of the
input specified and is commonly used in conjunction with COUNT. Before
seeing it in action, let's add another row to our table so that the results of
using DISTINCT jump out clearly (Listing 8-3).

Listing 8-3. Inserting a new row in our programming languages
table

```
INSERT INTO proglang_tbl
 (id, language, author, year, standard)
VALUES
 (6, 'PL/I', 'IBM', 1964, 'ECMA');
```

Note the new data choice that we are populating with our new
row. With PL/I we now have a fourth distinctive standards organization –
ECMA. PL/I also shares the same birth year as APL (1964) giving us a
duplicate *year* field. Now let us run a query to check what distinct *year*
values we have in the table (Listing 8-4).

Listing 8-4. Distinct year values in the table

```
SELECT DISTINCT year
FROM proglang_tbl;
```

_____

Year

_____

1972

1988

1987

1964

1959

_____

Both 1964 and 1959 make an appearance only once as we desired. A common use case for DISTINCT is to combine it with the COUNT function to output the number of unique values we have in the table (Listing 8-5). Attempting the same for *year*, we get our expected result of 5.

Listing 8-5. Counting distinct year values

```
SELECT COUNT (DISTINCT year)
FROM proglang_tbl;

> 5
```

Using DISTINCT on the standard field has a slightly different output than we might expect at first guess (Listing 8-6).

Listing 8-6. Listing distinct standard values

```
SELECT DISTINCT standard
FROM proglang_tbl;
```

---

standard

(null)

ECMA

ANSI

ISO

US-DOD

We actually get five rows in our output including the null value because for the DISTINCT clause, it is a uniquely separate value. Combining this with COUNT removes the significance of the null row giving us the value 4 (Listing 8-7).

Listing 8-7. Counting distinct standard values

```
SELECT COUNT (DISTINCT standard)
FROM proglang_tbl;

> 4
```

Column Aliases

Queries are frequently consumed directly as reports since SQL provides enough functionality to give a meaningful representation to the data stored inside a RDBMS. One of the features allowing this is *Column Aliases*, which let you rename column headings in the resultant output. The general syntax for creating a column alias is given below (Listing 8-8).

Listing 8-8. General syntax for creating column aliases

```
SELECT <column1> <alias1>,
       <column2> <alias2>,
        ...
FROM <table>;
```

79

For example, we wish to output our programming languages table with a few columns only. But we do not wish to call the authors of the language as *authors*. The person wanting the report wishes they be called *creators*. This can be simply done by using the query below (Listing 8-9).

Listing 8-9. Renaming the author field to creator for reporting purposes

```
SELECT id,
       language,
       author creator
FROM proglang_tbl;
```

id	language	creator
1	Prolog	Colmerauer
2	Perl	Wall
3	APL	Iverson
4	JOVIAL	Schwartz
5	APT	Ross
7	Tcl	Ousterhout
6	PL/I	IBM

While creating a column alias will not permanently rename a field, it will show up in the resultant output. Implementations differ on whether they allow column aliases to be used in other parts of the query other than column listing. For example, let's try using the column alias *creator* in the WHERE clause of a query in PostgreSQL (Listing 8-10).

Listing 8-10. Using column aliases in the WHERE clause in PostgreSQL

```
SELECT id,
       language,
       author creator
FROM proglang_tbl WHERE creator = 'Ross';

ERROR:  column "creator" does not exist
LINE 4: FROM proglang_tbl WHERE creator = 'Ross';
```

Aha, PostgreSQL explicitly told us that this is a no-go. Let's see if SQLite is slightly more forgiving (Listing 8-11).

Listing 8-11. Using column aliases in the WHERE clause in SQLite

```
sqlite> SELECT id,
            language,
            author creator
        FROM proglang_tbl
        WHERE creator='Ross';

id          language    creator
----------  ----------  ----------
5           APT         Ross
```

While SQLite did allow it, I'm not really fond of using column aliases in anything other than column renaming for the output. I'd advise that you do the same unless there is a very strong case of readability improvement and your implementation allows it (and there are very few that allow it).

Order of Execution of SELECT Queries

A query is not evaluated from left to right; there is a specific sequence in which its various parts are evaluated as given below.

1. FROM clause

2. WHERE clause

3. GROUP BY clause

4. HAVING clause

5. SELECT clause

6. ORDER BY clause

There is an interesting corollary of having the SELECT evaluation being lower than the WHERE clause. Can you guess what it is?

It is the inability of database management systems like PostgreSQL, DB2, and Microsoft SQL Server to use column aliases in the WHERE clause. Until the point the query execution is on the filtering stage using the conditions provided, it has still not resolved the column aliases of the query.

Let's test this by running a query in PostgreSQL where we use the column alias in the ORDER BY clause, the only one with a lower precedence (Listing 8-12).

Listing 8-12. Using column aliases in the ORDER BY clause

```
testdb=# SELECT id,
       language,
       author creator
FROM proglang_tbl
ORDER BY creator;
```

```
 id | language |  creator
----+----------+------------
  1 | Prolog   | Colmerauer
  6 | PL/I     | IBM
  3 | APL      | Iverson
  7 | Tcl      | Ousterhout
  5 | APT      | Ross
  4 | JOVIAL   | Schwartz
  2 | Perl     | Wall
(7 rows)
```

Our reasoning was rewarded with the correct output, not that I would change my advice of using column aliases only with proper thought.

Using the LIKE Operator

While putting conditions on a query using WHERE clauses, we have already seen comparison operators = and IS NULL. Now we take a look at the LIKE operator, which will help us with wildcard comparisons. For matching we are provided with two wildcard characters to use with LIKE.

- **% (Percent)** Used to match multiple characters including a single character and no character

- **_ (Underscore)** Used to match exactly one character

We will first use the % character for wildcard matching. Let us suppose we wish to list out languages that start with the letter **P** (Listing 8-13).

Listing 8-13. All languages starting with P

```
SELECT * FROM proglang_tbl
WHERE language LIKE 'P%';
```

id	language	author	year	standard
1	Prolog	Colmerauer	1972	ISO
2	Perl	Wall	1987	
6	PL/I	IBM	1964	ECMA

The output of the above query is all language records whose name begins with the letter capital P. While we don't have such a record, note that this resultset would not include any language that starts with the small letter p.

We can see that using the % wildcard allowed us to match multiple characters like *erl* in the case of Perl. But what if we wanted to restrict how many characters we wished to match? What if our goal was to write a query that displays the languages ending in the letter l, but are only three characters in length? The first condition could have been satisfied using the pattern %l, but to satisfy both conditions in the same query we use the _ wildcard. A pattern like %l would result in returning both *Perl* and *Tcl*, but we modify our pattern suitably to return only the latter (Listing 8-14).

Listing 8-14. All languages ending with l and 3 characters long

```
SELECT * FROM proglang_tbl
WHERE language LIKE '__l';
```

id	language	author	year	standard
7	Tcl	Ousterhout	1988	

Note that the result did not include *Perl* since we explicitly gave two underscores to match two characters only. Also it did not match *APL* or *JOVIAL* since SQL data is case sensitive and l is not equal to L.

We can also use NOT in conjunction with LIKE to negate or inverse the result. If we used a NOT in the conditional clause of Listing 8-14, what languages do we expect to get back in the result? Having *Perl, APL,* and *JOVIAL* is certainly right, but they are not the entire resultset. Any language that is not three characters long and ending with a lowercase l would be in the output (Listing 8-15).

Listing 8-15. Using NOT with LIKE

```
SELECT * FROM proglang_tbl
WHERE language NOT LIKE '__l';
```

id	language	author	year	standard
1	Prolog	Colmerauer	1972	ISO
2	Perl	Wall	1987	
3	APL	Iverson	1964	ANSI
4	JOVIAL	Schwartz	1959	US-DOD
5	APT	Ross	1959	ISO
6	PL/I	IBM	1964	ECMA

Be careful when using LIKE; its comparisons are computationally expensive on the database, especially the ones involving multiple % wildcards.

CHAPTER 9

Calculated Fields

We have already seen *column aliases* that allow us to rename a field's name in the query output. But we frequently encounter conditions that require changes to a field value. This is where the concept of a *calculated field* comes in.

Mathematical Calculations

Any numeric field can be operated upon by mathematical operators we are all familiar with. We can add, subtract, multiply, divide, and even find the remainder of a division operation fairly easily. While the operators supported differ in various implementations, the ones given below should be available across any RDBMS you come across (Table 9-1).

Table 9-1. *Mathematical Operators Available in SQL*

Addition	+
Subtraction	-
Multiplication	*
Division	/
Remainder	%

© Rahul Batra 2018
R. Batra, *SQL Primer*, https://doi.org/10.1007/978-1-4842-3576-8_9

Let us take our programming languages table and try to find out the decade in which the language was created. For example, Prolog was created in the 1970s decade. Let us try to find out this fact from the year of creation available to us. One approach is to find the remainder of the year when divided by 10, which is the number of years in a decade (Listing 9-1). This is the value that specifies how many years it has been since the start of that decade.

Listing 9-1. Using the remainder operation

```
SELECT language,
       (year % 10) remain
FROM proglang_tbl;
```

language	remain
Prolog	2
Perl	7
APL	4
JOVIAL	9
APT	9
Tcl	8
PL/I	4

Now if we subtract this value from the year of creation itself, we would get the decade in which the programming language was created (Listing 9-2).

Listing 9-2. Finding the creation decade of a language

```
SELECT language,
       year - (year % 10) decade
FROM proglang_tbl;
```

language	decade
Prolog	1970
Perl	1980
APL	1960
JOVIAL	1950
APT	1950
Tcl	1980
PL/I	1960

Another approach is to divide the year by 10 and then multiply it by 10. This is slightly less straightforward because it relies on the definition of the `integer` data type. Since an integer cannot store decimal points, division by 10 would silently chop off the remainder. The year 1972 divided by 10 would be 197 discarding the .2 bit. If we multiply this value by 10, we would get our desired decade value (Listing 9-3).

Listing 9-3. Finding the creation decade of a language using an alternative calculation

```
SELECT language,
       (year / 10) * 10 decade
FROM proglang_tbl;
```

String Operations

By far the most commonly used string operation is *concatenation*. It means to join or combine strings. However, since even numeric fields can be treated as a string, we can use the concatenation operator || on them too. See the example below to modify our *decade* field to include some characters (Listing 9-4).

Listing 9-4. Using the string concatenation operator

```
SELECT language,
       'The '||((year/10)*10)||'s' decade
FROM proglang_tbl;
```

language	decade
Prolog	The 1970s
Perl	The 1980s
APL	The 1960s
JOVIAL	The 1950s
APT	The 1950s
Tcl	The 1980s
PL/I	The 1960s

Note that the concatenation operator manifests itself in different forms in different implementations. PostgreSQL, SQLite, and Oracle use the shown || symbols whereas Ingres, MySQL, and Microsoft SQL Server use + to denote concatenation. Their effect, however, is the same.

The string concatenation operator differs in various programming languages too. The || character, which is used in most SQL implementations, comes from the IBM PL/I – a language quite popular in the '60s and '70s but rarely seen in modern times.

The last character I actually is the roman numeral for 1, as it was built purposely to unify the growing gap between languages specializing in business processes and those catering to scientific computation.

Another common string operation is *substring*, which returns only a part of the string field value. For example, if we needed to get only the first two characters of each programming language, we would use the SUBSTR function. The general syntax of this function is given below (Listing 9-5).

Listing 9-5. General syntax of substring

```
SELECT SUBSTR(<field name>, <starting position>, <length>),
        ...
FROM <table>;
```

The *starting position* is the character you wish to start extracting from. Unlike most programming languages, the string index positions here don't start from 0 but 1. The third argument *length* specifies how many characters should be a part of the result. For the first two characters of a programming language, the starting position would be 1 and the length would be 2 (Listing 9-6).

Listing 9-6. Extracting the first two characters of a programming language

```
SELECT SUBSTR(language, 1, 2),
        year
FROM proglang_tbl;
```

substr	year
Pr	1972
Pe	1987
AP	1964
JO	1959
AP	1959
Tc	1988
PL	1964

Interestingly, on one hand, PostgreSQL gives the same result when we use SUBSTRING instead of SUBSTR, because it treats them as aliases. SQLite, however, works only with SUBSTR. Microsoft SQL Server, on the other hand, works only with SUBSTRING. Check your database manual for which version your implementation expects.

Another class of string operations that often comes in handy are UPPER and LOWER, which change the case of a string value to upper- and lowercase respectively. This is best illustrated with an example (Listing 9-7).

Listing 9-7. Changing the case of fields

```
SELECT UPPER(language),
       LOWER(standard)
FROM proglang_tbl;
```

upper	lower
PROLOG	iso
PERL	
APL	ansi
JOVIAL	us-dod
APT	iso
TCL	
PL/I	ecma

Literal Values

There are cases when one needs to use a fixed literal value as the values of a new column. Like column aliases can change the column header for readability, literal values change record values. In a sense they are not calculated fields, but fixed fields inserted in specific positions of a record.

An example will help illustrate this – supposing you wish to really clarify the year of language creation, as not just a number but also to include the characters AD (Listing 9-8).

Listing 9-8. Using literal values

```
SELECT language,
       year,
       'AD'
FROM proglang_tbl;
```

language	year	AD
Prolog	1972	AD
Perl	1987	AD
APL	1964	AD
JOVIAL	1959	AD
APT	1959	AD
Tcl	1988	AD
PL/I	1964	AD

We can even use numeric literal values the same way, omitting the quotation marks for such values. A common utility for literal values arises when the user has to copy-paste data from their database query output into another tool like a spreadsheet or word processor.

CHAPTER 10

Aggregation and Grouping

SQL has maintained its prominent position in the technical world due to its ability to cater to a wide range of business intelligence and analytic requests. While databases are often used for finding a needle in a haystack, that is, narrowing down to a single row, a lot of interactive usage of SQL revolves around generating aggregated insights from a bunch of rows.

Indeed, a major advantage that SQL-based systems have over NoSQL data storage solutions is how intuitive grouping and aggregation is in the former category.

Aggregate Functions

An *aggregate function* is used to compute summarization information from a table or tables. We have already seen the COUNT aggregate function that counts the records matched. Similarly, there are other aggregation functions in SQL like AVG for calculating averages; SUM for computing totals; and the extreme functions MAX, MIN for finding out maxima and minima values respectively.

The count and extreme functions work with all data types, but functions like SUM and AVG make sense only with numeric types and thus work only with them.

© Rahul Batra 2018
R. Batra, *SQL Primer*, https://doi.org/10.1007/978-1-4842-3576-8_10

Let's now try to use AVG on the only sensible numeric choice we have in our table – *year* (Listing 10-1). You can think of the below query as a way of finding out the mean year value of all the programming language records we have in our table.

Listing 10-1. Finding the Average year of creation in our programming languages table

```
1.  SELECT AVG(year) FROM proglang_tbl;
```

avg
1970.4285714285714286

We can see the result as a decimal number with a default of 16 digits after the decimal point in PostgreSQL. This is slightly lowered to 10 digits after the decimal point in SQLite but more than enough still to cover all but the rare scenarios.

While the average value was calculated accurately, one can argue that a value like this to specify *year* is not useful. What we really want is a readable year value that looks like an actual year, an integer value specifically. Thus we go about *casting* this average value to an integer (Listing 10-2).

Listing 10-2. Casting values to integers

```
SELECT CAST(AVG(year) AS INTEGER)
FROM proglang_tbl;
```

avg
1970

Conversion of data types using CAST only works with compatible data types like numerics and integers. If you try to convert a *varchar* into an *integer*, the DBMS will spit out an error message as is proper (Listing 10-3).

Listing 10-3. Casting incompatible types

```
testdb=# SELECT CAST(language AS INTEGER)
        FROM proglang_tbl;

ERROR:  invalid input syntax for integer: "Prolog"
```

The exception here is SQLite, which will obediently convert the *varchar* value to 0. This may be the most sensible choice for it because of its underlying engine implementation; however, I would warn you to stay away from such surprising cast operations.

Let's try the other numeric aggregate function that is commonly used – SUM. Suppose we wish to find the sum of the *year* values in our table – the query would be written in a straightforward way using SUM (Listing 10-4).

Listing 10-4. Using the SUM aggregate function

```
SELECT SUM(year)
FROM proglang_tbl;
```

sum
13793

As before, if we use SUM on a varchar field, PostgreSQL would spit out an error while SQLite would quietly give a value of 0.0 (Listing 10-5).

Listing 10-5. Using SUM on a varchar field in PostgreSQL

```
testdb=# SELECT SUM(language)
        FROM proglang_tbl;

ERROR:  function sum(character varying) does not exist

LINE 1: SELECT SUM(language) FROM proglang_tbl;
                   ^

HINT:  No function matches the given name and argument types.
You might need to add explicit type casts.
```

Using the Extreme Functions – MAX and MIN

MAX and MIN are collectively called the extreme functions because they essentially find the extreme values from a set of column values. Their most intuitive application is with numeric data, but these functions can be applied to other database types as well.

These functions are fairly straightforward to understand and use. Let's take the MIN first. It looks at a particular set of rows and finds the minimum value of the column that is provided as an argument to it. For example, in our table we wish to find out from which year do we have records of programming languages, that is, the earliest language year. Analyzing the problem at hand, we see that if we apply the aggregate function MIN to the field *year* in our table, we should get the desired output (Listing 10-6).

Listing 10-6. Using the MIN extreme aggregate function

```
SELECT MIN(year)
FROM proglang_tbl;
```

min
1959

We had two languages in our table corresponding to the year 1959 – *APT* and *JOVIAL*. But since this is the minimum value, it was the result once regardless of how many languages had the same value. The function MAX is similar, but its result would signify the latest year in which one of the languages in our table was created (Listing 10-7).

Listing 10-7. Using the MAX extreme aggregate function

```
SELECT MAX(year)
FROM proglang_tbl;
```

max
1988

Of course you can combine them in a single query to get the result in a single row itself (Listing 10-8).

Listing 10-8. Using MAX and MIN together

```
SELECT MAX(year),
       MIN(year)
FROM proglang_tbl;
```

max	min
1988	1959

Like we read before, these functions are not limited to numeric types. So let's combine finding the MAX *year* value with the MIN *language* value (Listing 10-9).

Listing 10-9. Mixing MAX and MIN types

```
SELECT MAX(year),
       MIN(language)
FROM proglang_tbl;
```

max	min
1988	APL

The `MIN` language found was *APL* since it's the first alphabetically. Notice that *APT* was not chosen since L < T when comparing alphabets.

We need to be careful while reading this result though. At first glance it gives a misleading view that *1988* corresponds to *APL*, which is not the case. Our query simply gives the extreme values of these two fields in our table, whether they are from the same record or not.

Grouping Data

The `GROUP BY` clause of a `SELECT` query is used to *group records* based upon their field values. This clause is placed after the `WHERE` conditional. For example, in our sample table we can group data by which committee decided on their standard. Let's see this action after we insert another record in our table so that the logical nature of grouping becomes clearer (Listing 10-10).

Listing 10-10. Grouping records by its fields

```
INSERT INTO proglang_tbl
 (id, language, author, year, standard)
VALUES
 (8, 'Fortran', 'Backus', 1957, 'ANSI');
```

```
SELECT standard FROM proglang_tbl
WHERE standard IS NOT NULL
GROUP BY standard;
```

standard
ECMA
ANSI
ISO
US-DOD

Notice how the different standards are *grouped* into a single value, regardless of how many times they occur in the table. Let's try to add the *language* column to the output of the above query (Listing 10-11).

Listing 10-11. Trying to add language to our output fields

```
SELECT standard,
       language
FROM proglang_tbl
WHERE standard IS NOT NULL
GROUP BY standard;
```

ERROR: column "proglang_tbl.language" must appear in the GROUP BY clause or be used in an aggregate function

The database engine gave us an error for this query. This makes sense because while it bunched the different standards together because of our grouping clause, which language it should choose to display with it is ambiguous. Let us take the error message's first suggestion and also include the *language* field in the GROUP BY clause (Listing 10-12).

Listing 10-12. Adding language to our output fields

```
SELECT standard,
       language
FROM proglang_tbl
WHERE standard IS NOT NULL
GROUP BY standard, language;
```

standard	language
ECMA	PL/I
ANSI	APL
US-DOD	JOVIAL
ISO	Prolog
ISO	APT
ANSI	Fortran

The interesting thing to note here is the rule that the columns listed in the SELECT clause must be present in the GROUP BY clause. This leads us to the following two corollaries.

1. You cannot group by a column that is not present in the SELECT list.

2. You must specify all the columns in the grouping clause that are present in the SELECT list.

Bare Columns in SQLite   If you tried executing Listing 10-11 in SQLite, you would not get an error. This is because of the *bare column* feature in SQLite that allows a column to be present without aggregation in the SELECT clause and still be absent from the GROUP BY clause.

This is quite different from most DBMS systems out there, and I would suggest that you stay away from using this feature seriously because of the undefined behavior involved. However, it is good to read up on the details present at the SQLite website.

```
https://www.sqlite.org/lang_select.html
```

Grouping and Aggregate Functions

Another useful way to use grouping is to combine the operation with an aggregate function. Suppose we wish to count how many standards a particular organization has in our table. This can be achieved by combining the GROUP BY clause with the COUNT aggregate function as given below (Listing 10-13).

Listing 10-13. Using GROUP BY with aggregate functions

```
SELECT standard,
       COUNT(*)
FROM proglang_tbl
GROUP BY standard;
```

standard	count
<null>	2
ECMA	1
ANSI	2
ISO	2
US-DOD	1

The output is intuitive enough to warrant no further explanation, but the query itself is interesting. Notice that the GROUP BY clause consisted of only the *standard*. The aggregate function is a result of the bunching of the grouped columns.

Grouping truly makes sense in SQL when used judiciously with aggregate functions. A lot of utility and intelligence from databases are derived from analysts using a combination of these applied on a well-designed model. Let's see another example of combining GROUP BY with multiple aggregate functions this time.

Suppose we wish to find out how many languages were made in the same year, and of those languages which come first alphabetically (Listing 10-14). We can immediately see that a GROUP BY on *year* is needed here along with a couple of different aggregate functions.

Listing 10-14. Using GROUP BY with multiple aggregate functions

```
SELECT year,
       MIN(language),
       COUNT(*)
FROM proglang_tbl
GROUP BY year;
```

year	min	count
1972	Prolog	1
1957	Fortan	1
1988	Tcl	1
1987	Perl	1
1964	APL	2
1959	APT	2

The HAVING Clause

Like a WHERE clause places conditions on the fields of a query, the HAVING clause places conditions on the groups created by GROUP BY. It must be placed immediately after the GROUP BY but before the ORDER BY clause (Listing 10-15).

Listing 10-15. Demonstration of the HAVING clause

```
SELECT language,
       standard,
       year
FROM proglang_tbl
GROUP BY standard,
         year,
         language
HAVING year < 1980;
```

language	standard	year
APT	ISO	1959
JOVIAL	US-DOD	1959
APL	ANSI	1964
Fortran	ANSI	1957
PL/I	ECMA	1964
Prolog	ISO	1972

From the output we can clearly see that the records for Perl and Tcl are left out since they do not satisfy the HAVING conditional of being created before 1980.

You might wonder why we need two different filtering clauses – WHERE and HAVING. A WHERE clause does not allow aggregate functions in its conditionals, a prime target for the HAVING clause. For example, suppose we wish to check which *standard* values exist more than once in our table. Our first stab at this using the GROUP BY clause might look something like this (Listing 10-16).

Listing 10-16. Trying aggregate functions in WHERE

```
SELECT standard
FROM proglang_tbl
WHERE COUNT(standard) > 1
GROUP BY standard;

ERROR:  aggregate functions are not allowed in WHERE
```

Just like we thought, our SQL interpreter did not allow such a travesty. Instead we'll use the same conditional in the HAVING clause (Listing 10-17).

Listing 10-17. HAVING clause with aggregate functions

```
SELECT standard
FROM proglang_tbl
GROUP BY standard
HAVING COUNT(standard) > 1;
```

standard
ANSI
ISO

It correctly gave us the names of the two *standard* values with more than one occurrence. Interestingly, if we tweak the conditional to COUNT(*), we get an additional row (Listing 10-18).

Listing 10-18. Changing the aggregate function behavior

```
SELECT standard
FROM proglang_tbl
GROUP BY standard
HAVING COUNT(*) > 1;
```

standard
(null)
ANSI
ISO

The filtering clause is now not restricted to non-null values of the *standard* column. Since there are multiple records with null values in the field, it will also be included in the result.

CHAPTER 11

Understanding Joins

A *join* operation allows you to retrieve data from multiple tables in a single SELECT query. Two tables can be joined by a single join operator, but the result can be joined again with other tables. There must exist a same or similar column between the tables being joined.

When you design an entire database system using good design principles like *normalization*, we often require the use of joins to give a complete picture to a user's query. For example, we split our programming languages table into two in Chapter 7 – one holding the author details (Table 11-2) and the other holding information about the languages itself (Table 11-1). To show a report listing authors and which programming language they created, we would have to use a join.

Table 11-1. *Contents of newlang_tbl*

id	language	year	standard
1	Prolog	1972	ISO
2	Perl	1987	(null)
3	APL	1964	ANSI
4	Tcl	1988	(null)
5	BASIC	1964	ANSI

© Rahul Batra 2018
R. Batra, *SQL Primer*, https://doi.org/10.1007/978-1-4842-3576-8_11

Table 11-2. *Contents of authors_tbl*

author_id	author	language_id
1	Colmerauer	1
2	Wall	2
3	Ousterhout	4
4	Iverson	3
5	Kemeny	5
6	Kurtz	5

We now form a query to show our desired output – the list of all authors with the corresponding language they developed (Listing 11-1). We choose our join column as the *language_id* field from the authors table. This corresponds to the *id* field in the languages table.

Listing 11-1. Running a join operation on our two tables

```
SELECT author, language
FROM authors_tbl, newlang_tbl
WHERE language_id = id;
```

author	language
Colmerauer	Prolog
Wall	Perl
Ousterhout	APL
Iverson	Tcl
Kemeny	BASIC
Kurtz	BASIC

The output of our query combines a column from both tables giving us a better report. The language_id = id is called the *join condition*. Since the operator used in the join condition is an equality operator (=), this join is called an *equijoin*. Another important thing to note is that the columns participating in the join condition are not the ones we choose to be in the result of the query.

Remember that the joining of tables to view a resultset does not affect the tables at all. Nothing physically changes in the tables themselves with respect to their structure or data. The implicit connection forming is only within the lifetime of the join query execution.

Alternative Join Syntax

You would have noticed that we formed our join query without much special syntax, using our regular FROM/WHERE combination. The SQL-92 standard introduced the JOIN keyword to allow us to form join queries. Since it was introduced earlier, the FROM/WHERE syntax is still quite popular for joins. But now that the majority of database vendors have implemented most of the SQL-92 standard, the JOIN syntax is also in widespread use. Below is the JOIN syntax equivalent of the query we just wrote to display which author created which programming language (Listing 11-2).

Listing 11-2. Rewriting our query using the JOIN(SQL-92) syntax

```
SELECT author, language
FROM authors_tbl JOIN newlang_tbl
ON language_id = id;
```

Notice that instead separating the two tables using a comma (thereby making it a list), we use the JOIN keyword. The columns that participate in the join condition are preceded by the ON keyword. The WHERE clause can then be used after the join condition specification (ON clause) to specify any further conditions if needed.

The kind of joins where all rows that don't match the join condition exactly are eliminated are called *inner joins*. Thus we can optionally use the full keyword INNER JOIN in our queries without affecting the resultset (Listing 11-3).

Listing 11-3. Specifying INNER JOIN explicitly

```
SELECT author, language
FROM authors_tbl INNER JOIN newlang_tbl
ON language_id = id;
```

Resolving Ambiguity in Join Columns

In our example the join condition fields had distinct names – *id* and *language_id*. But what if in our languages table we kept the key field's name as *language_id*? This would create an ambiguity in the join condition, which would become the confusing language_id = language_id. To resolve this, we need to qualify the column by prepending it by the table name it belongs to and a .(period) (Listing 11-4).

Listing 11-4. Resolving the naming ambiguity by qualifying the columns

```
CREATE TABLE languages_tbl
 (language_id INTEGER, language VARCHAR(20));

INSERT INTO languages_tbl VALUES (4, 'Tcl');

SELECT author, language
FROM authors_tbl JOIN languages_tbl
ON language_id = language_id;
```

```
=> ERROR:  column reference "language_id" is ambiguous

SELECT author, language
FROM authors_tbl JOIN languages_tbl
ON authors_tbl.language_id = languages_tbl.language_id;
```

author	language
Ousterhout	Tcl

Another way to solve such ambiguity is to qualify the columns using *table aliases*. The concept is to give a short name to a table and then use this to qualify the columns instead of a long, unwieldy table name (Listing 11-5).

Listing 11-5. Using table aliases

```
SELECT author, language
FROM authors_tbl a JOIN newlang_tbl l
ON a.language_id = l.id;
```

Here the authors table is given the alias a and the languages table is given the alias l. It is generally considered a good practice to qualify column names of a join condition regardless of whether there is a name ambiguity or not.

Outer Joins

Since we encountered *inner joins* in Listing 11-3, it gave us a clue to the existence of *outer joins*. In this kind of join, the resultset consists of rows that match the join condition and the rows that don't match the condition from one of the tables. If the rows from the first table that don't match the condition are desired in the resultset, we use a *left outer join*. Otherwise when rows from the second table are required, we use a *right outer join*.

113

This sounds a bit confusing at first, so let's clarify the concept using an example. Let's add a single row to the *newlang_tbl* about the Lisp programming language, but we will not make any entry into the authors table for this (Listing 11-6).

Listing 11-6. Adding a new row to illustrate outer joins

```
INSERT INTO newlang_tbl
VALUES (6, 'Lisp', 1958, 'ANSI');
```

If we ran an inner join query on the two tables like Listing 11-1, we would get a similar output as the query gave that time around. This new row we added would not feature in the resultset. But let's try a left outer join where we explicitly want this new row to be in the results despite not having an entry in the authors table. Our first table must then be the *newlang_tbl* and the query would be as below (Listing 11-7).

Listing 11-7. A left outer join example

```
SELECT language, author
FROM newlang_tbl n LEFT OUTER JOIN authors_tbl a
ON n.id = a.language_id;
```

language	author
Prolog	Colmerauer
Perl	Wall
APL	Ousterhout
Tcl	Iverson
BASIC	Kemeny
BASIC	Kurtz
Lisp	

Aha, success! The LEFT OUTER JOIN allowed us to sneak the Lisp row into the resultset with a null *author* value. Looking at the query listing, if you immediately think that just by switching the order of the joined tables, we can convert this into a RIGHT OUTER JOIN, then you are absolutely right (Listing 11-8).

Listing 11-8. A right outer join example

```
SELECT language, author
FROM authors_tbl a RIGHT OUTER JOIN newlang_tbl n
ON n.id = a.language_id;
```

The output of this query would be exactly the same as in Listing 11-7. Notice that our join condition specified in the ON clause did not need any order change. Since all right outer joins can be written as left outer joins (and vice versa), it is rare to find many real-world usages of right outer joins. SQLite goes as far as not support right outer joins at all, which is just as well.

Cross Joins

You might think what would happen if we left out the join condition from our query. Well what happens in the background of running a join query is that first all possible combinations of rows are made from the tables participating in the join. Then the rows that satisfy the join condition are chosen for the output (or further processing). If we leave out the join condition, we get as the output all possible combinations of records (Listing 11-9). This is called a *Cross Join* or *Cartesian Product* of the tables usually denoted by the sign X.

115

Listing 11-9. Query for showing the cartesian product of our tables

```
SELECT author, language
FROM authors_tbl, newlang_tbl;
```

author	language
Colmerauer	Prolog
Colmerauer	Perl
Colmerauer	APL
Colmerauer	Tcl
Colmerauer	BASIC
Colmerauer	Lisp
Wall	Prolog
Wall	Perl
Wall	APL
Wall	Tcl
Wall	BASIC
Wall	Lisp
Ousterhout	Prolog
...	...

The output of the query is truncated here, but when you run it on your computer you should get 36 rows in the result containing each *author* and *language* combination. Another way to rewrite this query is to actually use the JOIN keyword with a preceding argument CROSS as shown below (Listing 11-10).

Listing 11-10. Rewriting our query using CROSS JOIN

```
SELECT author, language
FROM authors_tbl CROSS JOIN newlang_tbl;
```

Notice the lack of the ON clause, which means no join condition.

What if we were selecting more than one column from the *newlang_tbl*, say both *language* and *year*? Would the number of combinations increase dramatically from our cross join above? Turns out that no, the number of records in the resultset would be exactly the same as before (Listing 11-11). A cartesian product is the combination of records from the tables participating in the joins, not within the unit of record for a single table.

Listing 11-11. Selecting multiple columns from a table participating in a cross join

```
SELECT author, language, year
FROM authors_tbl CROSS JOIN newlang_tbl;
```

author	language	year
Colmerauer	Prolog	1972
Colmerauer	Perl	1987
Colmerauer	APL	1964
...	...	...

A cross join is not something you would come across often. It is of some utility when either of the tables is small, that is, consisting of a few rows, and you need a combination of all the values of it joined with a bigger table. However I'd advise against running cross joins on actual production database servers unless you really understand why you need them in the scenario.

Self Joins

Sometimes a table within its own columns has meaningful data but one (or more) of its fields refer to another field in the same table. For example, if we have a table in which we capture programming languages that influenced other programming languages and denote the influence relationship by the language id, to show the resolved output we would have to join the table with itself. This is also called a *self join*. Consider the table created below and pay close attention to the data being inserted (Listing 11-12).

Listing 11-12. Creating and populating our language influence table

```
CREATE TABLE inflang_tbl (id INTEGER PRIMARY KEY,
                          language VARCHAR(20) NOT NULL,
                          influenced_by INTEGER);

INSERT INTO inflang_tbl (id, language)
 VALUES (1, 'Fortran');

INSERT INTO inflang_tbl (id, language, influenced_by)
 VALUES (2, 'Pascal', 3);

INSERT INTO inflang_tbl (id, language, influenced_by)
 VALUES (3, 'Algol', 1);
```

id	language	influenced_by
1	Fortran	
2	Pascal	3
3	Algol	1

Our goal is to now write a self join query to display which language influenced which one, that is, resolve the *influenced_by* column (Listing 11-13).

Listing 11-13. Running a self join query

```
SELECT l1.id,
       l1.language,
       l2.language AS influenced
FROM inflang_tbl l1, inflang_tbl l2
WHERE l1.id = l2.influenced_by;
```

id	language	influenced
3	Algol	Pascal
1	Fortran	Algol

Notice the use of table aliases to qualify the join condition columns as separate and the use of the AS keyword that renames the column in the output.

What if we wanted to use the alternative SQL-92 JOIN syntax for our self join? Well as it turns out, there is no special self join keyword or clause because it is not needed. To the SQL query interpreter, you have created an inner join on two tables who just happen to have exactly similar contents. So we can rewrite the Listing 11-13 query using our familiar JOIN keyword as below (Listing 11-14).

Listing 11-14. Running a self join query using JOIN

```
SELECT l1.id,
       l1.language,
       l2.language AS influenced
FROM inflang_tbl l1 JOIN inflang_tbl l2
ON l1.id = l2.influenced_by;
```

Non-Equi Joins

The joins we have seen till now have largely dealt with equality in their join
condition. While this is the most common way of joining tables together,
we are by no means restricted to use only equality. Let's put another join
condition between the *newlang_tbl* and *authors_tbl* between the *id* and
author_id this time (Listing 11-15).

Listing 11-15. A non-equi join

```
SELECT id,
       author_id,
       author,
       language
FROM authors_tbl, newlang_tbl
WHERE id < author_id;
```

id	author_id	author	language
1	2	Wall	Prolog
1	3	Ousterhout	Prolog
2	3	Ousterhout	Perl
1	4	Iverson	Prolog
2	4	Iverson	Perl
3	4	Iverson	APL
1	5	Kemeny	Prolog
2	5	Kemeny	Perl
3	5	Kemeny	APL
4	5	Kemeny	Tcl
1	6	Kurtz	Prolog

id	author_id	author	language
2	6	Kurtz	Perl
3	6	Kurtz	APL
4	6	Kurtz	Tcl
5	6	Kurtz	BASIC

While not the most logical of results, it does however satisfy our non-equality join condition that in each row the *id* field is lesser than the corresponding *author_id* field value. We can also freely mix this result with an equality condition using the familiar AND operator within the same query (Listing 11-16).

Listing 11-16. Using the equality and non-equality conditions

```
SELECT id,
       author_id,
       author,
       language
FROM authors_tbl, newlang_tbl
WHERE id < author_id
AND id = language_id;
```

id	author_id	author	language
3	4	Iverson	APL
5	6	Kurtz	BASIC

The result now consists of records where the author of a language has their *author_id* value greater than their created languages' *id*.

CHAPTER 12

Subqueries

A *subquery*, simply put, is a query written as a part of a bigger statement. Think of it as a SELECT statement inside another one. The result of the inner SELECT can then be used in the outer query. Let us take a simple example to illustrate this.

Consider the same source tables as the ones in the joins chapter – *authors_tbl* and *newlang_tbl*. We will try to write a query (and a subquery) to display the author of a particular language (Listing 12-1).

Listing 12-1. A simple subquery example

```
SELECT author FROM authors_tbl
 WHERE language_id IN
 ( SELECT id FROM newlang_tbl
   WHERE language="Tcl");
```

author
Ousterhout

The subquery SELECT id FROM newlang_tbl WHERE language='Tcl' picks the correct language id from the *newlang_tbl* and passes it on to the outer query on the authors table. This frees us from the responsibility of joining the two tables using the language *id* field.

© Rahul Batra 2018
R. Batra, *SQL Primer*, https://doi.org/10.1007/978-1-4842-3576-8_12

We can visualize the intermediate step where the subquery has already resolved to a value. The query would now look something like `SELECT author FROM authors_tbl WHERE language_id IN (4)`.

Which approach to take in certain situations – a join, a subquery, or a combination of both – is mostly a matter of personal preference. Other times, one approach will be clearly the superior choice. Remember that all joins can be rewritten as subqueries, but the reverse is not true in all cases.

Types of Subqueries

We can broadly classify subqueries into three categories.

1. **Scalar subqueries** A subquery that returns only a single column of a single row as its output. The example in the previous section, where the subquery returns the `id` for *Tcl*, is a scalar subquery.

2. **Row subqueries** A subquery that returns a single row but more than one column. These are the least important type of subqueries since most database management systems do not support it, including SQLite.

3. **Table subqueries** A table subquery can return more than a single row and many columns per row. In essence, it can return a table itself to take part in your outer query.

To illustrate the usage of table subqueries, let us take an example where we wish to display all the programming language writers who created a language after 1980 (Listing 12-2).

Listing 12-2. A table subquery example

```
SELECT author, language
FROM authors_tbl a,
     (SELECT id, language
      FROM newlang_tbl
      WHERE year > 1980) n
WHERE a.language_id = n.id;
```

author	language
Wall	Perl
Ousterhout	Tcl

Carefully study the FROM clause of the query above. Our table subquery is placed within it, and it returns a set of languages that were created after 1980. The result consists of two rows and two columns, one of which, that is, *language* is picked up to be displayed in the final output.

Existence Tests in Subqueries

The keyword EXISTS tests the presence of any number of rows returned from a subquery. We usually don't care about the columns being returned by the mere existence of rows satisfying a specific criterion. Let's try to use EXISTS test to display languages who have an author entry in the *authors_tbl* (Listing 12-3).

Listing 12-3. Using an existence test

```
SELECT language,
       year
FROM newlang_tbl
WHERE EXISTS (SELECT * FROM authors_tbl
              WHERE newlang_tbl.id = language_id);
```

language	year
Prolog	1972
Perl	1987
APL	1964
Tcl	1988
BASIC	1964

Notice the subquery WHERE clause in this case. It is effectively referencing the outer table field using newlang_tbl.id. For whichever languages this existence test will be satisfied, the outer query will add to the resultset.

We can add the option NOT to the existence test to find the complement of the result (Listing 12-4).

Listing 12-4. Using NOT in the existence test

```
SELECT language,
       year
FROM newlang_tbl
WHERE NOT EXISTS (SELECT * FROM authors_tbl
                  WHERE newlang_tbl.id = language_id);
```

language	year
Lisp	1958

Recall that we had never put the corresponding entry in the authors table for Lisp in the last chapter.

So who created Lisp anyway?   Lisp is the second oldest programming language whose major dialect is still in active use. John McCarthy created Lisp in 1958 as a part of his research, and other people chipped in to help implement it on the computers of that era.

McCarthy by all accounts was a genius-level intellect, widely admired by his peers. He was one of the pioneers of the field of Artificial Intelligence and even coined the term. With the creation of Lisp, he advanced the field of programming language design by leaps and bounds. Over the past three decades, features from Lisp are slowly trickling into mainstream programming languages. Many renowned technologists still marvel at the design of the decades-old Lisp dialects – Common Lisp and Scheme.

Though McCarthy died in 2011 at the age of 84, his legacy and work lives on.

Using Subqueries in INSERT Statements

We can even use subqueries inside other SQL statement like INSERT. Let us try to add a new language and a new author in our tables and ease our task of remembering *id* numbers by just a bit by using subqueries (Listing 12-5).

Listing 12-5. Inserting a new programming language

```
INSERT INTO newlang_tbl
 (id, language, year, standard)
VALUES (7, 'Pascal', 1970, 'ISO');
```

The updated content of our programming languages table now looks as shown below (Table 12-1).

Table 12-1. *Contents of newlang_tbl*

id	language	year	standard
1	Prolog	1972	ISO
2	Perl	1987	
3	APL	1964	ANSI
4	Tcl	1988	
5	BASIC	1964	ANSI
6	Lisp	1958	ANSI
7	Pascal	1970	ISO

While inserting a new entry into the *authors_tbl*, we can either remember that we used the *language_id* as 7 for Pascal or use a subquery. Let us see an example of the latter approach (Listing 12-6). After all, the title of the chapter gave away our approach!

Listing 12-6. Inserting a new author using a subquery

```
INSERT INTO authors_tbl
 (author_id, author, language_id)
VALUES (7, 'Wirth',
        (SELECT id FROM newlang_tbl WHERE language="Pascal")
       );
```

We believe that this should put the correct language id for Mr. Wirth since he created Pascal. Let us verify this belief by looking at the contents of the table.

author_id	author	language_id
1	Colmerauer	1
2	Wall	2
3	Ousterhout	4
4	Iverson	3
5	Kemeny	5
6	Kurtz	5
7	Wirth	7

You can even use subqueries to control your UPDATE and DELETE statements. The logic remains much the same as with using subqueries in SELECT and INSERT.

Using ANY and ALL

The ANY operator used with the arithmetic comparison operators can be used to check a column value in comparison to a similar value(s) generated in the subquery. For example, if we wanted to display all the languages but exclude the oldest one from the result, we could combine > and ANY to achieve this (Listing 12-7).

Listing 12-7. Using the ANY operator

```
SELECT language
FROM newlang_tbl
WHERE year > ANY (SELECT year FROM newlang_tbl);
```

language
Prolog
Perl
APL
Tcl
BASIC
Pascal

Only Lisp does not have a creation year that is not greater than *any* of the list of values returned by the subquery. Obviously, this is because the smallest value returned is the creation year of Lisp itself, and thus it does not feature in the final result.

Now what would happen if we reversed our comparison operator to < ANY? The result would include all languages whose *year* value is less than any one of the creation years returned by the subquery (Listing 12-8).

Listing 12-8. Using the ANY operator with <

```
SELECT language
FROM newlang_tbl
WHERE year < ANY (SELECT year FROM newlang_tbl);
```

language
Prolog
Perl
APL
BASIC
Lisp
Pascal

We notice that Lisp has snuck into the resultset but Tcl is notably absent. This is because the *year* of Tcl, that is, 1988 is not less than any of the values returned by the subquery. Equal to? Sure, but not distinctly less than.

The other comparison conjunction we can use with ANY is =, but that is rarely seen because it is equivalent to using IN (), which is much more intuitive.

SQLite does not support ANY or ALL operators   If you tried running the above examples in SQLite, you would get an error message as below.

Error: near "SELECT": syntax error

SQLite currently does not support these keywords, but we can still achieve the same results using what we have to work with. Let's attempt to rewrite Listing 12-7 displaying all languages but the oldest one.

SELECT language FROM newlang_tbl

WHERE year <> (SELECT MIN(year) FROM newlang_tbl);

The above query computes our desired resultset just fine and is pretty readable. Some, including yours truly, actually prefer it to the ANY syntax. If you are wondering about <>, it means not equal to.

The ALL operator works similarly, but the value in the WHERE clause must hold true for *all* of the values returned from the subquery (Listing 12-9). One scenario where ALL gets usage is to find data related to extreme values like minima and maxima. You are of course free to choose the built-in functions MAX and MIN for the purpose too.

Listing 12-9. Using the ALL operator

```
SELECT language
FROM newlang_tbl
WHERE year <= ALL (SELECT year FROM newlang_tbl);
```

language

Lisp

Only Lisp being the oldest language in our table would satisfy the ALL criteria of having a *year* value less than or equal to all the values from the subquery. Similarly, we can use ALL to find the latest language too (Listing 12-10).

Listing 12-10. Using the ALL operator with >=

```
SELECT language
FROM newlang_tbl
WHERE year >= ALL (SELECT year FROM newlang_tbl);
```

language

Tcl

CHAPTER 13

Working in Sets

Set theory is a branch of discrete mathematics that deals with a collection of objects. There is a lot of conceptual overlap between set theory and relational database concepts. It is no wonder that the output of a query is frequently called a result**set**.

Primitive set theoretic operations like *union, intersection*, and *difference* are increasingly supported in various implementations. We will now explore the theory behind these operations and how to use them in SQL.

Union

The *union* is an operation that combines elements of two sets. Let's say we have the following two sets consisting of a bunch of numbers (Listing 13-1).

Listing 13-1. Two sets containing numbers

```
set1 = { 1, 3, 5 }

set2 = { 1, 2, 3 }
```

The resulting union set will be a set consisting of all of these elements repeated exactly once, that is, no duplicates are allowed (Listing 13-2). Note that the order of a set is unimportant. Think of it as a bag of elements rather than an ordered collection.

© Rahul Batra 2018
R. Batra, *SQL Primer*, https://doi.org/10.1007/978-1-4842-3576-8_13

Listing 13-2. The mathematical UNION operation

```
set1 UNION set2 = { 1, 3, 5, 2 }
```

Let's now look at how to use simulate the union operation in SQL. Consider our programming languages table and its data below as we last left it in Chapter 10 (Table 13-1).

Table 13-1. *Contents of proglang_tbl*

id	language	author	year	standard
1	Prolog	Colmerauer	1972	ISO
2	Perl	Wall	1987	
3	APL	Iverson	1964	ANSI
4	JOVIAL	Schwartz	1959	US-DOD
5	APT	Ross	1959	ISO
6	PL/I	IBM	1964	ECMA
7	Tcl	Ousterhout	1988	
8	Fortran	Backus	1957	ANSI

If we wanted to get the list of creation years of languages standardized by either ANSI or ISO, we could use a UNION keyword to achieve this (Listing 13-3).

Listing 13-3. Using a UNION operator

```
SELECT year FROM proglang_tbl
 WHERE standard='ANSI'
UNION
SELECT year FROM proglang_tbl
 WHERE standard='ISO';
```

year
1959
1957
1964
1972

Since we had four entries in our table with a *standard* value as ANSI or ISO, we got our expected four rows in the resultset. Note that there were no duplicate entries to be processed. But what if there were duplicate entries to process with the UNION operation (Listing 13-4)?

Listing 13-4. Using a UNION operator to eliminate duplicate values

```
SELECT standard FROM proglang_tbl
 WHERE language = 'Fortran'
UNION
SELECT standard FROM proglang_tbl
 WHERE language = 'APL';
```

standard
ANSI

Both the languages we specified in our WHERE clause were standardized by ANSI. The UNION operation, just like in discrete maths, removed the duplicated value and gave out a single row as the result.

There is another related SQL operation UNION ALL that will simulate the act of combination but will not eliminate duplicates (Listing 13-5). The advantage you get by using this is performance improvement since the SQL engine does not have to bother with checking for duplicates. If you have constructed your participating queries in such a way that there are no repeated values, using a UNION ALL would improve your query processing time.

135

Listing 13-5. Using a UNION ALL operator

```
SELECT standard FROM proglang_tbl
 WHERE language = 'Fortran'
UNION ALL
SELECT standard FROM proglang_tbl
 WHERE language = 'APL';
```

standard
ANSI
ANSI

Intersection

The *intersection* operation outputs only the common elements in the input sets. If we apply an intersection to the two sets in the previous section, we get a resulting set of two elements (Listing 13-6).

Listing 13-6. The mathematical INTERSECTION operation

```
set1 INTERSECTION set2 = { 1, 3 }
```

As with union, each common value is displayed only once. Duplicates are removed from the final result set.

Translating this to SQL is pretty simple; instead of using UNION we use the keyword INTERSECT to get common elements (Listing 13-7).

Listing 13-7. Using the INTERSECT in SQL

```
SELECT standard FROM proglang_tbl
 WHERE year=1964
INTERSECT
SELECT standard FROM proglang_tbl
 WHERE year=1957;
```

standard
ANSI

Something to keep in mind here is that the INTERSECT operator would find the exact common values between the two queries that precede and succeed it. That means the entire records of the result and not just common values from a part of it. While in the previous example, our result set had only one column to be given back – *standard*, let's see what happens when we add another column to the result list (Listing 13-8).

Listing 13-8. Using the INTERSECT with multiple columns in the results

```
SELECT year, standard FROM proglang_tbl
 WHERE year=1964
INTERSECT
SELECT year, standard FROM proglang_tbl
 WHERE year=1957;
```

```
=> (0 rows)
```

The output is no rows at all. The first query would select records for PL/I and APL while the second for Fortran. But all these languages have a different combined value of *(year, standard)*, giving us a net zero result.

Note that while the ANSI SQL standard does provision for an INTERSECT ALL operator, I'm yet to come across a database management system that implements it. PostgreSQL happily ignores that you wrote the ALL clause and simply gives back an INTERSECT result.

Difference

The *difference* operation between sets, written as set1 - set2 is a list of all elements in *set1* that do not occur in *set2* (Listing 13-9). If an element is only in *set2*, it will not be captured by the plain difference operation.

Listing 13-9. The mathematical DIFFERENCE operation

```
set1 DIFFERENCE set2 = { 5 }
set2 DIFFERENCE set1 = { 2 }
```

Let's try and write a SQL statement to emulate this logic with our familiar IN and NOT IN operators. But first let's insert a row into our table so that we can see the difference operation in action (Listing 13-10).

Listing 13-10. Inserting a new row for RPG

```
INSERT INTO proglang_tbl
 (id, language, author, year, standard)
VALUES

 (9, 'RPG', 'IBM', 1964, 'ISO');
```

Suppose we wish to list out the years of creation of languages that were standardized by ISO but not the ANSI (Listing 13-11). From our source table, we find that three languages were standardized by ISO with years 1972, 1959, and 1964. But since in 1964, APL was created, which was eventually standardized by ANSI, we should ideally be left with the answer 1972 and 1959.

Listing 13-11. Trying to write set difference with IN

```
SELECT year FROM proglang_tbl
  WHERE standard IN ('ISO')
    AND standard NOT IN ('ANSI');
```

year
1972
1959
1964

Whoa, what sorcery is this!?! We thought 1964 would be ineligible because of ANSI standardization. But clearly this is not the case. What has happened actually is that first there was a scan of ISO rows – giving us three values. Then ANSI rows were discounted but not necessarily from the first result but the table as a whole. So while the APL 1964 was left off, the freshly inserted RPG 1964 still remained, effectively making our second condition worthless. The correct way to achieve this is using the set difference operator EXCEPT as below (Listing 13-12).

Listing 13-12. Set difference with EXCEPT

```
SELECT year FROM proglang_tbl WHERE standard IN ('ISO')
EXCEPT
SELECT year FROM proglang_tbl WHERE standard IN ('ANSI');
```

year
1972
1959

Voila, this seems to yield the correct answer! If you happen to be using an Oracle system, replace EXCEPT with MINUS to achieve the exact same result.

When we write more than a single SELECT as a part of a single query and join them using a set theoretic operator, such statements are called *compound queries*. Do note that many database management systems restrict the use of compound queries as subqueries. Sybase Adaptive Server Enterprise is one such popular DBMS that doesn't allow you to write a UNION inside a subquery.

CHAPTER 14

Views

One of the beautiful aspects of the relational data model and SQL is that the output of a query is also a table, a relation to be precise. It may consist of a single column or a single row, but it is a table nonetheless. A *view* is a query that can be used like a table.

Think of it as a *virtual table* that stores for the viewer's convenience a pre-computed resultset. It does not truly exist like a *base table* but provides a different angle to view the data without the tedium of details.

Why Are Views Needed?

Most production database systems would contain a lot of tables. It is also possible that some of these tables consist of a lot of fields because of the complexity of the domain. Views would come to the rescue of the casual database user, people who are not experts in all parts of the database system. They have a specific, repetitive need, and views provide them with a simpler interface to the data they need.

Another advantage that views bring to the table is security. We can restrict access to base tables and provide views containing only the data a particular group of users is allowed to see. Good database design rules often force sensitive columns to be lumped together with oft-accessed fields. Views come to the rescue in such cases by effectively hiding the sensitive columns if you so choose.

© Rahul Batra 2018
R. Batra, *SQL Primer*, https://doi.org/10.1007/978-1-4842-3576-8_14

For the database designers, views provide independence. To a reasonable degree, views allow the underlying base tables to change their structure to cater to evolving needs and yet views can remain the same. In other cases, views can be re-created with a different query underlying it but will contain the same data in the same format, providing a continuity to the user.

Creating a View

The general syntax of creating a view is pretty straightforward (Listing 14-1). In fact, it probably is as minimal and natural as you can get.

Listing 14-1. General syntax of view creation

```
CREATE VIEW <view name> AS <query>
```

Now let us create a view for ourselves – *language_chronology* that will have only two fields, namely, languages and their years of creation (Listing 14-2).

Listing 14-2. Creating a language_chronology view

```
CREATE VIEW language_chronology AS
 SELECT language, year
 FROM proglang_tbl
 ORDER BY year ASC;
```

Notice how we have explicitly added the ordering clause to the view creation. There are very few restrictions on what is allowed in the query part of CREATE VIEW. Let us now verify the results by running a query on the view exactly the same way as we would on a table (Listing 14-3).

Listing 14-3. Listing the contents of a view

```
SELECT * FROM language_chronology;
```

language	year
Fortran	1957
JOVIAL	1959
APT	1959
RPG	1964
APL	1964
PL/I	1964
Prolog	1972
Perl	1987
Tcl	1988

We can also include calculated fields in the query part of view creation. The only thing we must keep in mind is how we rename the calculated field column, failing which would undoubtedly result in a loss of clarity. Let's re-create our decade query from Chapter 9, this time as a view (Listing 14-4).

Listing 14-4. Creating a view with a calculated field

```
CREATE VIEW language_decade AS
  SELECT language,
         'The '||((year/10)*10)||'s' decade
  FROM proglang_tbl;
```

language	decade
Prolog	The 1970s
Perl	The 1980s
APL	The 1960s
JOVIAL	The 1950s
APT	The 1950s
Tcl	The 1980s
PL/I	The 1960s
Fortran	The 1950s
RPG	The 1960s

If we had failed to rename the column as *decade*, our DBMS systems would execute the view creation but the resultant view would be practically unusable. PostgreSQL would have renamed the column to a mysterious ?column? whereas SQLite would have put the entire expression as the name of the second field 'The '||((year/10)*10)||'s'. Needless to say, we are better off renaming the fields of the view.

Another way to rename the fields is to specify it in the view definition clause rather than the query that populates it (Listing 14-5). This works just as well and is arguably clearer because it lists the fields upfront.

Listing 14-5. Renaming the field in the view definition clause

```
CREATE VIEW language_era (lang, era) AS
 SELECT language,
        'The '||((year/10)*10)||'s'
 FROM proglang_tbl
 WHERE year < 1971;
```

lang	era
APL	The 1960s
JOVIAL	The 1950s
APT	The 1950s
PL/I	The 1960s
Fortran	The 1950s
RPG	The 1960s

If you choose this method of renaming columns, you must specify the names of all the columns in the view. Note that renaming a field has no effect on its data type or null status.

Modifying Data Through Views

There are widely ranging opinions on whether data modification through views is a good idea. Some people prefer to treat views as a read-only listing of contents, but most DBMS systems provide some data modification ability through views.

Let us first try a simple update of the *year* column through our *language_chronology* table (Listing 14-6). Remember we had pulled the *year* field into the view along with the language name.

Listing 14-6. Updating a value through a row

```
UPDATE language_chronology
SET year=1977
WHERE language='Fortran';
```

The statement executes fine in PostgreSQL. Now to verify whether it actually made a difference, let us verify the contents of the view first (Listing 14-7).

Listing 14-7. Checking contents of our modified view

```
SELECT * FROM language_chronology
WHERE language='Fortran';
```

language	year
Fortran	1977

All seems to be as expected in the view. While we have an inkling that the base table would also have been updated, let's verify this too (Listing 14-8).

Listing 14-8. Checking contents of our base table

```
SELECT * FROM proglang_tbl
WHERE language='Fortran';
```

id	language	author	year	standard
8	Fortran	Backus	1977	ANSI

This also means that the other view *language_era* that was dependent on *proglang_tbl* would not contain the row for Fortran since its creation involved the use of the condition WHERE year < 1971. Records move in and out of views as the underlying base table contents change over time.

View modification in SQLite   If you attempted to execute this UPDATE command in SQLite, it would throw you an error like:

```
Error: cannot modify language_chronology because it
is a view
```

SQLite has clearly stated that it would not stand for data modification through a view. A design choice I happen to agree with.

Let's attempt another data modification, but this time we will try to update the calculated field inside the view *language_era* (Listing 14-9). We know that JOVIAL was made in the year 1959, so we wish to round off the value and make its era to The 1960s.

Listing 14-9. Attempting to modify a calculated field of a view

```
UPDATE language_era SET era='The 1960s'
WHERE lang='JOVIAL';

> ERROR:  cannot update column "era" of view "language_era"

> DETAIL:  View columns that are not columns of their base
relation are not updatable.
```

The DBMS has rejected our request to update a calculated field because *era* does not exist in the base table *proglang_tbl*. If we think about it, this makes sense because the SQL interpreter would not know what *year* value to put in the base table. A value of 1960, a value of 1969, and everything in between would make the *era* value as The 1960s. The DBMS would not attempt to choose any random value because its reasoning would be ambiguous.

Changing the *lang* field of the same view is perfectly unambiguous and hence allowed (Listing 14-10).

Listing 14-10. Query to modify a non-calculated field of a view

```
UPDATE language_era SET lang='Jovial'
WHERE lang='JOVIAL';

> UPDATE 1

SELECT * FROM proglang_tbl
WHERE id=4;
```

id	language	author	year	standard
4	Jovial	Schwartz	1959	US-DOD

Similarly, we can create a view with aggregated columns using the GROUP BY clause, but modifying the contents of such a view is not allowed (Listing 14-11).

Listing 14-11. Creating a view with aggregate columns

```
CREATE VIEW standards AS
 SELECT standard, count(*)
 FROM proglang_tbl
 GROUP BY standard;
```

standard	count
	2
ECMA	1
ANSI	2
ISO	3
US-DOD	1

We know from previous experience that adding a new row or modifying the aggregated column would be ambiguous and thus not allowed. But what if we attempted to just update the *standard* field value just like we did with JOVIAL (Listing 14-12)? Would the update be reflected in all rows containing the field value?

Listing 14-12. Trying to modify a field value in an aggregated view

```
UPDATE standards SET standard='IS'
WHERE standard='ISO';

> ERROR:  cannot update view "standards"

> DETAIL:  Views containing GROUP BY are not automatically
updatable.

> HINT:  To enable updating the view, provide an INSTEAD OF
UPDATE trigger or an unconditional ON UPDATE DO INSTEAD rule.
```

The operation was disallowed but PostgreSQL gave us a hint on how to go about achieving this. While we won't cover that technique, it's good to know that in the rare case you do need it, it's available in some database systems.

Deleting Views

To delete or remove a view in its entirety, we use the DROP VIEW command. It is very similar to the DROP TABLE command we saw in Chapter 4 (Listing 14-13).

Listing 14-13. Dropping a view

```
DROP VIEW standards;
```

Note that you cannot accidentally drop a table using DROP VIEW, which is a relief (Listing 14-14).

Listing 14-14. Dropping a view

```
DROP VIEW proglang_tbl;

> ERROR:  "proglang_tbl" is not a view

> HINT:  Use DROP TABLE to remove a table.
```

CHAPTER 15

Indexing

Databases have long been the primary data storage components from which insights are derived. As businesses increasingly adopt technology-enabled workflows, the rate of data generation has grown substantially. This trend has accelerated with the adoption of the Internet and mobile computing.

A well-sized relational database used to run into hundreds of megabytes in the 1990s. It is not uncommon to hear of database systems running into hundreds of gigabytes or even a few terabytes nowadays. As a professional, you will frequently encounter tables with million rows in them.

Until now we have seen the parts of SQL that allow you to perform operations and run queries, but we haven't touched anything close to performance tuning. When you want to run your queries on multimillion record tables, taking a hard look at performance optimization is not optional.

One of the most common performance optimization techniques is indexing. An *index* allows the SQL engine to quickly *look up* specific records in a table. This is not unlike jumping directly to the letter W in a dictionary when you wish to know the meaning of *wistful*. It would be quite tedious to go through all the pages sequentially starting with A until we reach our desired word.

© Rahul Batra 2018
R. Batra, *SQL Primer*, https://doi.org/10.1007/978-1-4842-3576-8_15

A lot of commands in this chapter are specific to the DBMS at hand. While the general concept of indexes and basic commands to create and delete indexes remain similar across products, there is no getting around the fact that as we get deeper into our SQL journey, vendor-based differences become more visible.

Creating an Index

As with most statements in SQL, index creation is pretty straightforward. You use the CREATE INDEX command to achieve this (Listing 15-1).

Listing 15-1. General syntax of CREATE INDEX

```
CREATE INDEX <index name> ON <table name> (<column list>);
```

Let's create a simple index on the *language* column of *proglang_tbl* (Listing 15-2). We make a reasonable assumption that there are going to be a lot of queries using the *language* field in the WHERE clause, and creating an index on it would increase performance.

Listing 15-2. Creating an index on proglang_tbl

```
CREATE INDEX language_idx ON proglang_tbl(language);
```

If this command succeeds in *psql*, you would not get an error back but no other visual indication. Let's verify our index creation attempt by listing the table description like we did in Chapter 4. Instead of the detailed \d+ <table name> option, we will use the slightly compact \d <table name> command (Listing 15-3).

Listing 15-3. Verifying index creation in PostgreSQL

```
\d proglang_tbl;

          Table "public.proglang_tbl"
  Column  |          Type          | Modifiers
----------+------------------------+-----------
 id       | integer                |
 language | character varying(20)  |
 author   | character varying(25)  |
 year     | integer                |
 standard | character varying(10)  |

Indexes:
    "language_idx" btree (language)
```

We can see at the very end of the output, there is an entry for our index *language_idx*. Running the same CREATE INDEX on SQLite also succeeds, and there are two primary ways to verify the creation. The first is the .schema command we had seen in Chapter 4 (Listing 15-4).

Listing 15-4. Verifying index creation in SQLite using .schema

```
sqlite> .schema proglang_tbl

        CREATE TABLE proglang_tbl (
        id         INTEGER     NOT NULL,
        language   VARCHAR(20) NOT NULL,
        author     VARCHAR(25) NOT NULL,
        year       INTEGER     NOT NULL,
        standard   VARCHAR(10) NULL);

        CREATE INDEX language_idx ON proglang_tbl (language);
```

This showed us the DDL commands that were used to create the table and its related entities like indexes. Another approach is to use an SQLite *pragma* to list all indexes on a table (Listing 15-5). Pragmas are statements provided by SQLite to query its own metadata such as index information.

Listing 15-5. Verifying index creation in SQLite using a pragma

```
sqlite> PRAGMA index_list(proglang_tbl);

seq         name          unique      origin      partial
---------   ------------  ----------  ----------  ----------
0           language_idx  0           c           0
```

Using EXPLAIN to See Indexes at Work

We have now seen that the index we created actually exists, but how do we see it in action? We should be able to get a measurable speed up on a large table. The EXPLAIN command would come to our rescue here. But first let's go about creating a large table to run our index-enabled queries on.

A quick and dirty way to get a large table would be to use a cartesian product or cross joins. We already have our *proglang_tbl* with 5 columns and 9 rows in it. Doing a cartesian product on each of the fields with each other should yield us 9 to the power 5 = 59049 rows (Listing 15-6). This is not a huge table by any means but it would allow us to see the effect an index has on query execution.

Listing 15-6. Creating a big table using cross joins in PostgreSQL

```
SELECT a.language,
       b.author,
       c.year,
       d.standard,
       e.id
```

```
INTO biglang_tbl
FROM proglang_tbl a, proglang_tbl b, proglang_tbl c, proglang_
tbl d, proglang_tbl e;

SELECT count(*) FROM biglang_tbl;

 count
-------
 59049
```

Now that we have a populated table, let us try to analyze the query time for finding all Fortran rows using EXPLAIN (Listing 15-7). While this command is not in the SQL standard, most relational database systems implement it.

Listing 15-7. Using EXPLAIN on a query in PostgreSQL

```
EXPLAIN SELECT * FROM biglang_tbl WHERE language="Fortran";

                            QUERY PLAN
------------------------------------------------------------------
 Seq Scan on biglang_tbl  (cost=0.00..1150.11 rows=6486
 width=24)
   Filter: ((language)::text = 'Fortran'::text)
   (2 rows)
```

Well there is some output even though it is not entirely evident yet what we are seeing, A *query plan*, is a term for how the SQL engine is going to execute your query. Let us now contrast this output with the one after creating an index on the *language* field (Listing 15-8).

Listing 15-8. Using EXPLAIN on a query in PostgreSQL after creating an index

```
CREATE INDEX biglang_idx ON biglang_tbl (language);

EXPLAIN SELECT * FROM biglang_tbl WHERE language='Fortran';

                                    QUERY PLAN
---------------------------------------------------------------
----------------
 Bitmap Heap Scan on biglang_tbl  (cost=126.56..619.63
 rows=6486 width=24)
   Recheck Cond: ((language)::text = 'Fortran'::text)
   ->  Bitmap Index Scan on biglang_idx  (cost=0.00..124.94
       rows=6486 width=0)
         Index Cond: ((language)::text = 'Fortran'::text)
(4 rows)
```

We immediately see that this output is different from the previous one, and it involves the use of our recently created index. The previous output mentioned a Seq Scan or a sequential scan, which as the name suggests, involves going through our records sequentially. The current output, however, mentions Bitmap Heap Scan and Bitmap Index Scan, which sound way faster than a full simple scan. The details of how these particular scans work is out of the scope of this text, but we can look at another parameter in the output to get a relative sense of the efficiency of our index in this case.

Both plans mention a parameter-like cost=<1st value>..<2nd value>. The second value is the estimated total cost of query execution. The smaller this value is, the greater is the efficiency of query execution. In the first output without the index, this value is estimated as 1150.11 while after index creation, we reduce it down to 619.63, a big win for us.

While index creation on SQLite is similar to other databases, if you had tried to execute Listing 15-6 in it, you would have gotten an error saying something along the lines of `Error: near "INTO": syntax error`. The supported way to create the *biglang_tbl* in SQLite would be to use the `CREATE TABLE .. AS .. <query>` (Listing 15-9).

Listing 15-9. Creating the biglang_tbl in SQLite

```
CREATE TABLE biglang_tbl AS
 SELECT a.language,
        b.author,
        c.year,
        d.standard,
        e.id
 FROM proglang_tbl a, proglang_tbl b, proglang_tbl c,
      proglang_tbl d, proglang_tbl e;
```

Also instead of using the simple `EXPLAIN`, which gives a huge and pretty incomprehensible output at first glance, we use the more succinct `EXPLAIN QUERY PLAN` statement like below (Listing 15-10).

Listing 15-10. Using EXPLAIN QUERY PLAN in SQLite

```
EXPLAIN QUERY PLAN SELECT * FROM biglang_tbl WHERE
language="Fortran";
```

selectid	order	from	detail
0	0	0	SEARCH TABLE biglang_tbl USING INDEX biglang_idx (language=?)

While the output is pretty small as compared to the one from PostgreSQL, we can clearly see that it is going to use our index to search our table for Fortran rows.

Unique Indexes

We can optionally specify the keyword UNIQUE during index creation to make an index that only allows non-duplicate values (Listing 15-11). This makes the index have a dual responsibility of data integrity along with performance enhancement.

Listing 15-11. General syntax of UNIQUE index creation

```
CREATE UNIQUE INDEX <index name> ON <table name> (<column
list>)
```

However, since it has an implied data integrity meaning, we cannot use this kind of index on a field that is already known to have duplicate values. In our newly created *biglang_tbl*, the ID field is actually duplicated many times due to our cross join conditions. Creating a unique index on this field would result in an error (Listing 15-12).

Listing 15-12. Cannot create a unique index on a field containing duplicate values

```
CREATE UNIQUE INDEX id_idx ON biglang_tbl (id);

ERROR:  could not create unique index "id_idx"
DETAIL:  Key (id)=(4) is duplicated.
```

Similarly adding a duplicate value into a field that has a unique index would result in an error along the lines of ERROR: duplicate key value violates unique constraint "<index name>".

If you have an extremely sharp memory, you'd recall that this is the same error we saw in Listing 3-12 back in Chapter 3 when we were discussing unique constraints. If we now try to describe the schema of the involved table *proglang_tbluk*, we would see how PostgreSQL defined the constraints in terms of indexes (Listing 15-13).

Listing 15-13. Describing a table with both a Primary Key and a Unique index

```
\d proglang_tbluk;
            Table "public.proglang_tbluk"
     Column     |          Type          | Modifiers
----------------+------------------------+-----------
 id             | integer                | not null
 language       | character varying(20)  | not null
 author         | character varying(30)  | not null
 year           | integer                | not null
 standard       | character varying(10)  |
 current_status | character varying(32)  |
Indexes:
    "proglang_tbluk_pkey" PRIMARY KEY, btree (id)
    "proglang_tbluk_language_key" UNIQUE CONSTRAINT, btree
    (language)
```

Actually, this is also something we had tried in Chapter 4 in Listing 4-11, but we were not paying very close attention to the INDEXES section of the output back then.

How Do Indexes Work?

Having a high-level overview of how indexes work can help the user write effective, fast-executing queries. Most SQL users ignore the conceptual understanding of indexes, but they are not really hard to grasp.

At the beginning of the chapter, we compared the database index to looking up a word in a dictionary. That lookup process was made easier by the alphabetical ordering nature of a dictionary. Similarly a book index allows you to look up concepts discussed in the book by listing them alphabetically with a page number where the concept is discussed.

This is very similar to an actual database index. While the underlying details vary from implementation to implementation, it is helpful to think of it as an ordered lookup table. The values of the field being indexed are sorted and stored along with the pointers to the locations of the actual record in the base table.

If we created an index on the *standard* field of *proglang_tbl*, a simplified representation of the index would look like Figure 15-1. The SQL interpreter would not have to traverse through the whole of the table to find the two rows with ANSI as the standard field. The inefficient whole table traversal is what is sometimes referred to as full table scan or sequential scan. The point of an index is to avoid this kind of scan.

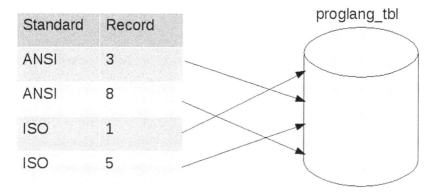

Figure 15-1. *A visual representation of the workings of an index*

When someone writes a query with a WHERE clause finding the specific value of a *standard*, this index would come into effect automatically without the user having to specify using it. Adding or deleting more rows with differing values of this field would automatically update the index too, so that the index always refers to the latest data in the table.

Index Overheads

With all the niceties that indexes bring to the user without much effort in terms of arcane commands, sometimes users want to create indexes for every column possible. After all, there doesn't seem to be a downside to index creation yet.

Well as it turns out, like with everything else in the world, there is no free lunch. If there is an index on every column for a table with N fields, then for every DML statement like INSERT, UPDATE, or DELETE, the N indexes have to be kept in sync. This makes changing data slow for large tables, sometimes annoyingly and sometimes worryingly.

Another serious overhead that too many indexes bring is their storage requirements. Indexes occupy physical space on the disk just like a table. While storage has become cheap in recent times, database administrators are not known for their cavalier attitude toward server free space.

Let's check how the disk is impacted by index creation. We will keep our focus on the *biglang_tbl* and its index *biglang_idx*. First let's find the total space occupied by the table and its related objects (Listing 15-14).

Listing 15-14. Displaying the total size of a table and its related objects in PostgreSQL

```
SELECT pg_size_pretty(pg_total_relation_size('biglang_tbl'));

 pg_size_pretty
----------------
 4608 kB
(1 row)
```

The function `pg_total_relation_size` would return the disk space occupied by the table, its indexes, and a few other things. The `pg_size_pretty` is for prettifying the output to a more human-readable unit of kB rather than the number of bytes. As is evident from these function names, they are specific to PostgreSQL. Check your DBMS manual for commands to query the database catalog in case you are using a different product.

Now let's find how much space the table and index take out of this figure (Listing 15-15). That should give us a relative idea about how big indexes get.

Listing 15-15. Displaying the size of a table and its index in PostgreSQL

```
testdb=# SELECT pg_size_pretty(pg_relation_size('biglang_tbl'));

 pg_size_pretty
----------------
 3296 kB
(1 row)

testdb=# SELECT pg_size_pretty(pg_relation_size('biglang_idx'));

 pg_size_pretty
----------------
 1312 kB
(1 row)
```

Our index is roughly 39% of the size of our table! Not to mention it occupies 28% of the total relation size of *biglang_tbl*. Keep in mind that we are talking about a single index on one column here. Clearly we need to be parsimonious with our index creation.

A good rule of thumb is to rely on the primary key and unique indexes a lot during your queries. Over time you will start seeing patterns of slow-running queries. If these queries are not run often, perhaps we can live with the extra time taken. But if the slow-running queries are run regularly and often contain the same field in the WHERE clause that is not indexed, it is a perfect candidate for index creation.

Index size in SQLite   You might have noticed that we discussed index sizes in PostgreSQL only. The helper functions like pg_size_pretty, pg_total_relation_size, and pg_relation_size are specific to PostgreSQL and are not a part of the SQL standard.

I haven't found a good way to calculate index sizes in SQLite. Since it is a self-contained single file database, you could verify the file size before and after index creation to get a rough estimate.

Deleting an Index

If you no longer need an index, SQL gives you the DROP INDEX command to delete an index. The general syntax of this command is simple enough (Listing 15-16).

Listing 15-16. General syntax of DROP INDEX

```
DROP INDEX <index name>
```

Note that this does not change the data of the underlying table in any way (Listing 15-17). All you are doing is dropping the index, so the query time may become slower.

Listing 15-17. DROP INDEX doesn't change the contents of the underlying table

```
DROP INDEX biglang_idx;
```

```
SELECT COUNT(*) FROM biglang_tbl;
 count
-------
 59049
(1 row)
```

CHAPTER 16

Access Control Statements

Due to their ease of use, extensive feature sets, and reliability, SQL-based relational database management systems have become the golden source of truth for enterprises everywhere. When large companies think of storing critical data, the only question in their minds is which relational DBMS vendor and not what kind of data store.

When such important data is being stored in the system and when the DBMS becomes the central data store across the organization, some level of access control is absolutely essential.

Access control refers to permissions within a software system. When you log onto a server or sometimes even your own computer, you have been given permission to access the resources of the system. Often when you wish to install new software on your machine, you require *root* or *administrator* privileges. This is the operating system's access control mechanisms at work.

Relational databases understandably also have very powerful access control mechanisms. While most systems vary widely in how they provide access control, almost all vendors do provide the Data Control Language (DCL) SQL commands of GRANT and REVOKE.

© Rahul Batra 2018
R. Batra, *SQL Primer*, https://doi.org/10.1007/978-1-4842-3576-8_16

Access Control in SQLite   Permissions truly come into play in multi-user systems, that is, when multiple users have access to a system but not equally. This is typically the case in client-server database systems like PostgreSQL, Sybase ASE, etc.

SQLite is a single file-based system typically used in scenarios where we need to embed a simple database within tight constraints or within an application. It is not truly meant for multi-user access though there are provisions in it to allow it to some degree. This does not mean that it is not a capable RDBMS. I personally think the world would be better off using SQLite in half the cases where more expensive and resource-hungry systems were put, but that is a discussion for another time.

SQLite being single file-based relies on the operating systems to grant or restrict access to its data file. Consequently, it does not implement any GRANT or REVOKE commands. The rest of the chapter focuses on access control mechanisms using PostgreSQL examples.

Creating New Users in PostgreSQL

For running the examples in the book, we have been using the user *postgres*. This has served us well as a catch-all account with all rights and permissions. Just to recap, we used to start our *psql* session by specifying the username in the -U option as below (Listing 16-1).

Listing 16-1. The psql session start command with user postgres

```
/opt/PostgreSQL/9.5/bin/psql -U postgres
```

But this does not accurately reflect the real-world setup. Usually you would have your own user account, which will have lesser privileges than the administrator account. This is safer both for you and the database administrators knowing that one account being compromised does not affect everything in the system.

Let us go about creating a new user in PostgreSQL though *psql* (Listing 16-2), and then we'll go on to specifying the rights that the particular user gets.

Listing 16-2. Creating a new user in psql

```
postgres=# CREATE USER primer with PASSWORD 'hunter2';

CREATE ROLE

postgres=#
```

When you execute this command, a new user by the name `primer` is created with the password `hunter2` and the console displays the message `CREATE ROLE`. Since the session was created with the user `postgres` and the text before the =# is still the same, we can see that the `CREATE USER` command does not switch to the new user directly but continues the same session with `postgres`.

The legend of hunter2   Before social networks were popular, Internet Relay Chat (IRC) ruled the instant messaging landscape. People connected to an IRC server and joined one or more chat rooms called channels and talked with like-minded people.

If a conversation was particularly funny, people would post it to a site Bash.org. Around 2004, somebody posted a funny exchange between two users where the first user convinces the other one that when they type their real password in IRC, everyone else sees only ******'s. This was of course not true, but funny nonetheless. Whether the conversation truly happened can also not be verified, but the password in question was 'hunter2'.

You can read the Bash.org entry here: `http://www.bash.org/?244321`

We will now try to verify whether the user was indeed created (Listing 16-3). Like before, *psql* gives us a short command for this – \du.

Listing 16-3. Checking if the user primer has been created

```
postgres=# \du
                         List of roles
  Role name |                  Attributes                    |
                               Member of
-----------+------------------------------------------------+
  postgres  | Superuser, Create role, Create DB, Replication,|
            | Bypass RLS                                     |
{}
  primer    |                                                |
{}
```

We see that indeed our user has been created, though the list of its attributes is empty. Don't worry, we will get to that in a bit.

If you want to verify the same information without using the *psql* metacommand, we can query the inbuilt database catalog information (Listing 16-4).

Listing 16-4. Querying user information from the database catalog

```
SELECT usename,
       usesysid,
       usecreatedb,
       usesuper FROM pg_user;
```

usename	usesysid	usecreatedb	usesuper
postgres	10	t	t
primer	41095	f	f

Grant Privileges to Users

Let us try to open a *psql* session using this newly created user. We will pass the value *primer* to the -U option of *psql* (Listing 16-5).

Listing 16-5. Trying to log in using our newly created user

```
/opt/PostgreSQL/9.5/bin/psql -U primer
Password for user primer:

psql.bin: FATAL:  database "primer" does not exist
```

Along with the user, it also tried to open the default database for the new user whose name was assumed to be the same as the username. We'll remedy this by explicitly stating that we want to operate on *testdb* (Listing 16-6).

Listing 16-6. Connecting to testdb using primer user

```
/opt/PostgreSQL/9.5/bin/psql -U primer -d testdb
Password for user primer:

psql.bin (9.5.8)
Type "help" for help.

testdb=> SELECT * FROM proglang_tbl;
ERROR:  permission denied for relation proglang_tbl
```

Logging into the testdb database worked. But when we ran a basic query on one of the tables, it immediately gave us a `permission denied` error. This seems logical in retrospect since we haven't granted any special access to *primer*. We don't want any new user to immediately gain access to our meticulously created tables.

We will use the GRANT statement to give specific privileges to our newly created user. The general syntax of GRANT is given below (Listing 16-7).

Listing 16-7. General syntax of GRANT

```
GRANT <privilege> ON <table name> TO <user>
```

The most obvious privilege we wish to give the *primer* user is the ability to query *proglang_tbl*. This is equivalent to giving the user a read-only access to the particular table. We run this statement as the superuser *postgres* who will bestow privileges to other users (Listing 16-8).

Listing 16-8. Granting SELECT to primer

```
GRANT SELECT ON proglang_tbl TO primer;
```

Now we can exit the *psql* session as *postgres* and reopen *testdb* as the user *primer*. We will attempt to first query and then update a row in the table just to see whether the GRANT statement worked as advertised (Listing 16-9).

Listing 16-9. Verifying whether primer can query or update the table

```
testdb=> SELECT count(*) FROM proglang_tbl;
 count
-------
     9
(1 row)

testdb=> UPDATE proglang_tbl SET year=1982 WHERE author='Ross';

ERROR:  permission denied for relation proglang_tbl
```

The query worked fine but the row update did not, so everything is working as expected. As you might have guessed, we would need to GRANT the UPDATE privilege too for the second statement to work.

SELECT and UPDATE are not the only privileges available for fine-grained access control. You can specify other privileges like INSERT and DELETE too. Finally, there is an ALL privilege that grants all the available privileges on that particular database object to the user specified. If you wish to specify multiple privileges in one go, you can specify them like a list (Listing 16-10).

Listing 16-10. Granting multiple privileges in one go

```
GRANT SELECT, UPDATE, INSERT ON proglang_tbl TO primer;
```

Granting privileges is usually done when the users who wish to access the table or database object in question are not the ones who created it. If a user has created a table, they get all privileges on it by default.

There are other privileges in most DBMS systems out there than the four basic ones we covered. However their use is usually of interest to the database administrators rather than query users. Feel free to refer to your DB manual to know more about the supported privileges.

Revoking Privileges

The REVOKE command is the exact opposite of GRANT. It allows you to remove privileges from a user for a database object. Its general syntax is similar to GRANT with the exception that it uses FROM instead of TO (Listing 16-11).

Listing 16-11. General syntax of REVOKE

```
REVOKE <privilege> ON <table name> FROM <user>
```

While discussing views in Chapter 14, we had mentioned how views help in data security by providing a virtual table containing only the fields you want to show to others. But this plan would be foiled if the users could query the base table too. Using REVOKE here is a good idea. We'd allow users to query the view but not the underlying table (Listing 16-12). This way we ensure that usability is not hampered while still being able to keep all kinds of fields together that make sense on a data-modeling level.

Listing 16-12. Revoking access on the base table

```
testdb=# GRANT SELECT ON language_decade TO primer;

testdb=# REVOKE SELECT ON proglang_tbl FROM primer;
```

We are running these commands using the superuser *postgres*. Let us now log in as the user *primer* and see how these statements have affected our privileges (Listing 16-13).

Listing 16-13. Checking privileges of the user primer

```
SELECT * FROM proglang_tbl;

ERROR:  permission denied for relation proglang_tbl

SELECT * FROM language_decade WHERE decade='The 1950s';
```

```
 language |  decade
----------+-----------
 Jovial   | The 1950s
 APT      | The 1950s
(2 rows)
```

We notice that the user can query the view but not the base table. This is in fact a very common access control workflow in large databases. Right after the data definition process, different views are created on the basis of how we expect the data to be queried, and then base table privileges are revoked for interactive querying.

While we can specify a list of users in GRANT and REVOKE, we cannot reasonably expect the list of users of a database system to remain the same over time. Most DBMS software provides a keyword PUBLIC to refer to all current and future users of a system. This can be used with our access control statements to minimize the need for routine access administration (Listing 16-14).

Listing 16-14. Using PUBLIC with access control statements

```
testdb=# GRANT ALL ON proglang_tbl TO PUBLIC;

testdb=# REVOKE DELETE ON proglang_tbl FROM PUBLIC;
```

What these two statements in succession would achieve is to first open up the *proglang_tbl* for everyone and then remove only the DELETE privilege. The other privileges like INSERT, UPDATE, etc., would be available to all users of the system without us having to list them one by one. If a new user is created, these access control levels would be applicable to them too.

APPENDIX A

Further Reading

This text was always meant to be a short, tutorial introduction to SQL for people who did not have prior experience with it. But this doesn't mean that we have learned all there is to learn about SQL. Indeed, we are far from it.

While I am happy that you got to the end of this text, it's only fair that I give you pointers on how to continue your SQL journey forward. Below is a list of books that I consider worthy of reading. Not all of them may suit you, so I am including a short description of what I felt about them to help you decide.

1. **The Practical SQL Handbook: Using SQL Variants (4th Edition, Addison-Wesley Professional, 2001)** *by Judith S Bowman, Sandra L Emerson, Marcy Darnovsky:* This is perhaps the best book on SQL that I have read, bar none. The writing is crisp, it is just the right size, and it focuses on the real-world aspects of SQL rather than too much obscure theory. The only downside is that it has not been updated since 2001; but since the basics of SQL change infrequently, coupling this with your database manual can help you get by swimmingly.

© Rahul Batra 2018
R. Batra, *SQL Primer*, https://doi.org/10.1007/978-1-4842-3576-8_17

2. **Introduction to SQL: Mastering the Relational Database Language (4th Edition, Addison-Wesley Professional, 2006)** *by Rick F van der Lans:* The gold standard in SQL references. Everything you ever wanted to know about SQL is covered in this heavy tome. The writing is a bit dry at times and the chapter organization might not suit complete beginners, but I don't think they were the intended audience anyways. I'd recommend you keep this handy if you frequently run into issues that Internet forums don't solve.

3. **SQL Queries for Mere Mortals: A Hands-On Guide to Data Manipulation in SQL (3rd Edition, Addison-Wesley Professional, 2014)** *by John L Viescas and Michael J Hernandez:* An extremely gentle but verbose tutorial on SQL in case you found the current text to be fast paced. The authors give a detailed step-by-step approach to translating plain English requirements to SQL queries. The examples are plentiful and is intended for complete beginners. This is a popular and well-regarded book and deservedly so.

4. **A Visual Introduction to SQL (2nd Edition, Wiley, 2001)** *by David Chappell and J Harvey Trimble Jr.:* Another classic that has not been updated for quite a while but is just as useful today. Meant as a visual tutorial introduction to SQL, it is to the point and covers a whole range of topics in 250 pages or so. A good choice to pick up from your library and go through in a month.

5. **Database Management and Design (2nd Edition, Prentice Hall, 1995)** *by Gary W Hansen and James V Hansen:* The hidden gem of the database theory book world. If you ever wanted to know the theoretical underpinnings of databases and SQL, this is text to read if you can find it. It is clearer and crisper than its more popular counterparts. It is unfortunate that there hasn't been a new edition in this millennium, and yet it still remains in my recommendation list. You would have to get past the outdated software that is used for examples in the book though.

6. **SQL Cookbook: Query Solutions and Techniques for Database Developers (1st Edition, O'Reilly Media, 2005)** *by Anthony Molinaro:* A superb collection of examples of real-world SQL queries. The book tries to cover all major DBMS packages and gives great explanations about the statements themselves. A great companion book if you are a working professional and frequently need to write queries that are not immediately obvious.

7. **The Art of SQL (1st Edition, O'Reilly Media, 2006)** *by Stephane Faroult and Peter Robson:* An advanced but fun way to look at SQL and relational databases. Modeled on Sun Tzu's Art of War, this book is distilled wisdom on how SQL-based databases ought to be used. This book immediately jumps into the nitty gritty of database design, performance optimization, and other such topics, so the reader is assumed to be well versed in the basics of SQL.

8. **SQL Antipatterns: Avoiding the Pitfalls of Database Programming (1st Edition, Pragmatic Bookshelf, 2010)** *by Bill Karwin:* This book is a crash course on what NOT to do while using SQL. You will learn to appreciate it after you have some experience under your belt, but a great book to browse through whenever you have time. The book is not too lengthy, roughly 300 pages, and is full of great tips on how to avoid bad database design and usage.

APPENDIX B

Database Management Systems and Tools

Ever since the 1980s there has always been a fair amount of choice in relational database management systems. But since the turn of the millennium, we now have ample choice in the open source world too. In fact, some of the strongest RDBMS tools are open source.

Below is a listing of my recommendations of good RDBMS systems and tools. It is biased toward free and open source software. Since it is an opinionated list by a single person, there are bound to be good resources that I have missed. Nonetheless, I hope this serves as a good starting point.

Relational Database Management Systems

1. **PostgreSQL** https://www.postgresql.org/ The best, most feature-rich open source database right now. It should be your default choice when trying to choose a RDBMS to be used by multiple programs and users. Its maturity and security are second to none and improvements trickle in at a steady pace.

© Rahul Batra 2018
R. Batra, *SQL Primer*, https://doi.org/10.1007/978-1-4842-3576-8_18

But its best feature for me is its documentation. The user manual that accompanies it serves as a great reference for SQL while being simple and succinct.

2. **SQLite** `https://sqlite.org/` A lightweight, single file, embeddable database. Extremely popular with lots of help and documentation available everywhere. Should be your choice of RDBMS when making a single user system or when the number of concurrent users is less. Does more than most people give it credit for, and it easily handles databases around 15–16GB in size.

3. **Firebird** `http://firebirdsql.org/` The hidden gem of the open source DBMS world. While not as well known as some of its peers, Firebird remains a stable, feature-rich and standard-compliant RDBMS. It scales well from small embeddable database systems to large, enterprise-wide ones. It began as a fork of Borland's Interbase in 2000 but now the two products have diverged quite a bit.

4. **MariaDB** `https://mariadb.org/` The community-developed fork of MySQL, now regarded as the default choice when looking for something that works like MySQL. There was a good ecosystem around MySQL that MariaDB automatically inherits and new features are being added to it on a regular basis.

5. **HyperSQL** `http://hsqldb.org/` Also known as HSQLDB, this is a popular, mature Java-based relational database engine. It can work both as an embedded and client/server-based DBMS. Perfect

for use with JVM languages. Think of it as an SQLite alternative in the Java universe, and just like SQLite it probably does a lot more than you expect it to.

6. **H2** `http://www.h2database.com` Another small, feature-rich Java-based database engine that can be used in embedded and client/server modes. It has similar design goals as HSQLDB but makes different trade-offs. In any case, you get an excellent, small, and open source database engine free of cost.

SQL Development Environments

Exploratory analysis of data stored inside relational databases has really picked up since the advent of the business intelligence and analytics fields. Consequently there is a new class of tools that allow you to interactively query your database and see the results in a nicely formatted manner.

Just like with RDBMS systems, you are spoiled for choice here. There are many free-to-use, open source SQL tools available. Some of them give even more features in their paid offerings, but for beginners the free versions go a long way.

1. **DBeaver** `https://dbeaver.jkiss.org/` My favorite SQL development environment. It is so full featured that I was surprised to know that it started out as a hobby project. Connects to many database systems and provides a plethora of features. However, all of this comes at a cost of speed and resources. Let's just say that if you have an old system, look elsewhere first.

2. **DB Browser for SQLite** `http://sqlitebrowser.org/` If you are working with SQLite, this is a top-notch data browser for it. It allows you to write queries and spits out a neatly formatted table too, but for most primitive operations like filtering on a column you don't need to write a query at all. Its browsing capabilities turn the tables into a spreadsheet-like abstraction allowing filtering of values.

A History of SQL and Relational Databases

Computers began their life as advanced calculating machines in the late 1940s and 1950s. But soon, businesses realized their importance in automated processing and recordkeeping. By the 1960s, computers increasingly used *file-oriented systems* to store data.

A typical workflow would consist of all related data stored as a single file and then an *application program* would operate on this file exclusively to provide an output. This operation would typically be done over night and there were multiple data files and multiple application programs working on them to support different data processing tasks.

The Rise of Sophisticated File-Oriented Systems

The very early computers used tape storage to store data. This meant that data access was restricted to *sequential scanning* of the records. You read the first record, then the next, and so on with no way to jump or go back without starting the read process from the very beginning. For application programs to process data stored in this fashion split in multiple files, they had to ensure that the data files were sorted by a specific field before the actual processing began. Doing this would enable a flow where the record read from one file would be in tandem with the records read from other files, and the complete information related to the record could be processed in one go.

With advancements in storage technology and the invention of magnetic disks and tapes, sophisticated data access methods also came around. Instead of simple sequential access, the *Indexed Sequential Access Method (ISAM)* became prominent in the 1960s. IBM developed ISAM and its successor *Virtual Storage Access Method (VSAM)* as file-oriented technologies allowing key-based direct access for its mainframe systems.

These systems were to be used with programming languages like COBOL and PL/I. Because of their integrated nature, they became popular in the enterprise environment and remained so for quite some time. However, a need for something more structured was already being felt.

The Entry of Database Systems

While the random access techniques did increase throughput, they never addressed another kind of problem that cropped up when organizations started moving multiple processes to automated data processing systems.

Data was split in multiple, independent files with no centralized logical structure in place. Redundant columns increased storage costs and the very real possibility of data inconsistency between various files. An even worse problem was data control with *homonyms* becoming inevitable. A homonym is created when the same field name is used for very different things in multiple files making a sensible understanding of the system an arduous task.

Logical data models and database systems arose to address some of the shortcomings of the file-oriented systems. They acted as integrated, centralized data structures that curbed the redundancy problem to a degree. An important concept that came around with database management systems was a *Data Dictionary* that provided meaning to the fields stored in the database. Suddenly everyone had access to a controlled, meaningful set of records thanks to a well-regulated data dictionary.

IBM released the *Information Management System (IMS)* in 1966 for use in the legendary NASA Apollo program. It was a *hierarchical database* that assumed all the data relationships can be structured as hierarchies. While the underlying data storage was still files tied together by pointers, IMS was a leap in data modeling where proper thought had to be given on how to best structure your data as a hierarchy.

Another kind of data model that picked up steam during the late 1960s was the *network data model.* It allowed you to represent data not just in a strict hierarchy but a complex network with entities referring to each other. This allowed for a more natural way of modeling data that was being generated in business processes. One of the earliest successful implementations of this model was the *Integrated Data Store (IDS)*, which started in 1964. It had such an impact on the industry that its design largely influenced the network model standard – the CODASYL DBTG standard.

Genesis of the Relational Model

While successful, the hierarchical and network models suffered from one inherent flaw in their design. Their modeling was driven from the viewpoint of a programmer with intricate knowledge of how they would interconnect multiple entities. Once the design was done, queries could be run as envisioned by the programmers with little chance for any further flexibility.

However Dr. Codd's relational theory proposed in 1970 insisted on not having rigid predetermined relationships through physical pointers. He believed that natural, logical relationships would manifest themselves by understanding the domain of the data and that the system should be ready for flexible querying. He built his model on sound mathematical theory rather than the intricacies of programming, which wasn't the case with what had come before.

The birthplace of relational databases was the IBM Research Labs at San Jose where Codd worked in the '70s and '80s. IBM came up with the *SystemR* project as a sort of a prototype relational database management system but failed to move fast enough in recognizing the gold they had struck. A company by the name of Relational Software Inc. created the first widely available industrial RDBMS in 1979 by borrowing IBM's research on SystemR. Relational Software Inc. went on to rename itself Oracle Corporation.

In the '70s, another project was drawing inspiration from SystemR but in an academic setting. Michael Stonebraker and Eugene Wong from the University of California, Berkeley, started their own research RDBMS called *Ingres*. It would prove to be Oracle's biggest competitor in the 1980s. While not as prevalent today as it once was, the Ingres project was tremendously impactful on the database industry as a whole. A lot of programmers who worked on it or read its easily available source code in the early years went on to subsequently contribute to other database systems.

The Hard Fought Battle of Query Languages

SQL wasn't the dominant query language of the early years of relational databases. In fact, Codd had proposed two early languages for data manipulation and querying – *relational algebra* and *relational calculus*. As is evident from the name, they were mathematical notations rather than attempts to make a query language with wide appeal.

Codd's attempt at making a real query language was *Alpha*, proposed in his 1971 paper "A Data Base Sublanguage Founded on the Relational Calculus." However, the SystemR project used a separate query language called *SEQUEL* created by Don Chamberlin and Raymond Boyce around 1973. This language eventually got renamed to *SQL*.

The Ingres project created their own query language called *QUEL*, influenced by the design of Alpha. However, in the 1980s the dominant vendors of database systems were pushing SQL, including IBM and Oracle, and QUEL died a slow death with the diminishing popularity of the trailblazing Ingres. By the late 1980s, SQL had firmly stamped its mark as the de facto database query language, a position it holds to this day.

Index

A

Access control, 165
    granting privileges to users
        general syntax, GRANT, 170
        multiple privileges, 171
    PostgreSQL, 166–169
    relational databases, 165
    REVOKE command, 172–173
    SQLite, 166
Aggregate functions
    AVG, 96
    casting values, integers, 96
    COUNT, 95
    MAX and MIN, 98–100
    SUM, 97–98
    varchar value, 97
Alpha, 187
ALTER TABLE command, 42–43
American National Standards
    Institute (ANSI), 3
The Art of SQL, 177
Atomicity, 67–68

B

Bitmap Heap Scan, 156
Bitmap Index Scan, 156

C

Check constraints, 30–31
Compound queries, 140
Concatenation operator, 89–90
Constraints
    check, 30–31
    NULL (*see* NULL constraints)
    primary key, 32–34
    relational databases, 25
    selective fields INSERT, 28–30
    unique key, 34–36
CREATE USER command, 167
Cross joins, 115–117

D

Database and database
    administrators (DBA's), 37
Database Management and
    Design, 177
Database Management System
    (DBMS), 1–3, 5, 8
Data Control Language
    (DCL), 5, 165
Data Definition Language
    (DDL), 5
Data Dictionary, 185

J, K

L

M

N

O

CPSIA information can be obtained
at www.ICGtesting.com
Printed in the USA
LVHW08s2033190918
590677LV00007B/68/P

9 781484 235751

33164300275174
November 2018